OLD POINT COMFORT RESORT

Nancy Powell
Williams
2020

A Hotel Chamberlin advertisement, circa 1907. *Courtesy of the Casemate Museum.*

OLD POINT COMFORT Resort

HOSPITALITY, HEALTH
AND HISTORY
ON VIRGINIA'S
CHESAPEAKE BAY

JOHN V. QUARSTEIN &
JULIE STEERE CLEVENGER

Charleston London

THE
History
PRESS

Published by The History Press
Charleston, SC 29403
www.historypress.net

First published 2009

Manufactured in the United States

ISBN 978.1.59629.485.1

Library of Congress Cataloging-in-Publication Data

Quarstein, John V.
Old Point Comfort resort : hospitality, health, and history on Virginia's Chesapeake
Bay / John V. Quarstein and Julia Steere Clevenger ; with photo editors J. Michael
Moore and Sara Johnston.
p. cm.
Includes bibliographical references and index.
ISBN 978-1-59629-485-1
1. Old Point Comfort (Hampton, Va.)--History. 2. Old Point Comfort (Hampton,
Va.)--Social life and customs. 3. Summer resorts--Virginia--Hampton--History. 4.
Seaside resorts--Virginia--Hampton--History. 5. Hotels--Virginia--Hampton--History.
6. Hampton (Va.)--History. 7. Hampton (Va.)--Social life and customs. 8. Cookery,
American--Southern style. 9. Cookery--Virginia--Hampton. I. Clevenger, Julie Steere.
II. Moore, J. Michael. III. Johnston, Sara. IV. Title.
F234.H23Q83 2009
917.55'412
2009026208

CONTENTS

FOREWORD

The Chamberlin Hotel has always been one of Hampton's most historical landmarks. It rises up from our shoreline and welcomes all to our community. Old Point Comfort was once America's greatest resort. Beginning with the Hygeia Hotel in 1822 and The Chamberlin in 1896, the resort's hotels thrived thanks to Hampton's marvelous sea breezes, outstanding transportation links, holiday atmosphere, memorable experiences, delicious food, historic sites and healthy climate. These same conditions remain today as The Chamberlin and Old Point Comfort prepare to grow in the twenty-first century.

The revitalized and restored Chamberlin is a wonderful community asset. Hampton is so fortunate that this magnificent building has been rehabilitated and renewed. It now stands as a symbol of how Fort Monroe's historical places can be cherished and reused. *Old Point Comfort Resort: Hospitality, Health and History on Virginia's Chesapeake Bay* shares with us the many stories on which we build today to make our future bright.

The Honorable Molly Joseph Ward
Mayor, City of Hampton

A NOTE FROM DRUCKER & FALK

When the Drucker & Falk team toured the Chamberlin Hotel in 1995, we were thoroughly taken aback and saddened by the building's deterioration. Age, hurricanes, neglect and the change in travelers' habits had taken their toll on this once magnificent old-world-style hotel. As I walked through the debris, my mind raced back to the days when I came to The Chamberlin for brunch with my family. It was always a fabulous experience. The food was scrumptious, and the building seemed so overwhelming in its size and grandeur. These memories made me realize how important it was to preserve The Chamberlin. This grand old hotel had to have a new life in the twenty-first century.

When we considered the building—its history, architecture, views and location—we realized that we could create a team to transform The Chamberlin into a spectacular adult-living community. Our dreams required a tremendous investment, over $50 million; yet through historic tax credits and with great determination, we were able to revive The Chamberlin. The Chamberlin is now a new experience, one that people can enjoy on a daily basis as a place to live and a place to gather. With Fort Monroe closing as a military installation, there will be opportunities to renovate other historical buildings on the base. Drucker & Falk believes that The Chamberlin is a vibrant example of what historic preservation can achieve.

When John Quarstein first approached us about this book, we realized that the stories of what once was America's premier resort had to be told. *Old Point Comfort Resort: Hospitality, Health and History on Virginia's Chesapeake*

Bay sheds light on the lifestyle of the past. The Chamberlin was a grand hotel, providing elegance and grace to its patrons through fine food and the freshness of the sea air. Memories of the dances, romance and gaiety, as well as visionary leadership and economic development, are part of the old Chamberlin's legacy. The revitalized Chamberlin epitomizes these stories for the modern world.

Wendy Drucker
CEO, Drucker & Falk

A REMEMBRANCE

The hotels on Old Point Comfort have always loomed large in the lives of the Phoebus community. Many residents worked for at least one of the hotels, and everyone recognized places like The Chamberlin as important gathering spots for social, political and military activities. After all, the town of Phoebus was named in honor of Harrison Phoebus, the owner of the fabulous second Hygeia. The Phoebus community always seems to grow after each remake of the Old Point Comfort hotels. It still continues today—isn't history amazing?

When I was young, only The Chamberlin still stood on Old Point Comfort; yet to me, it was the grandest place in Hampton Roads. I used to enjoy swimming in the saltwater pool or using our boats to sneak into big parties by way of the beach. The Roof Garden had the greatest dances, featuring bands like Terry and the Pirates, Bill Deal and the Rhondells and Adrian and the Sensations. It was all so much fun! Perhaps my fondest memory was when I would return from school in Baltimore aboard an Old Bay Line steamer. It was an overnight trip. We knew we were home when we awoke and looked out toward the horizon to see The Chamberlin glistening off in the distance, brightly reflecting the morning sun.

It was a sad day when I learned that The Chamberlin had closed its doors. Limited access onto Fort Monroe following 9/11 and bad management contrived to relegate The Chamberlin into a derelict. Fortunately, the Drucker & Falk firm stepped in to turn this once grand hotel into a marvelous adult community. The Chamberlin's rebirth is the beginning of Old Point

Comfort's revitalization. This adaptive-use story will occur again and again as Fort Monroe transitions to civilian ownership. Perhaps Old Point Comfort will once again become the leading resort in the South. I hope so.

The Honorable Ross A. Kearney
Member, Hampton City Council, 1992–2004, 2008–
Mayor, City of Hampton, 2004–2008

ACKNOWLEDGEMENTS

I will always remember my first visit to The Chamberlin in 1960. The hotel offered everything that I had started to value: historic view sheds, waterscapes, great food and significant architecture. As I began to learn more about Old Point Comfort, I gained an appreciation for its meaningful resort history. Even though I found Fort Monroe's military heritage so overwhelming, I simultaneously recognized how intertwined the fort once was with Hampton's tourism trade. The Coast Artillery Corps Band performed as young officers danced arm in arm with visiting damsels. It must have been a marvelous experience to be at Old Point Comfort in 1900.

Old Point Comfort Resort: Hospitality, Health and History on the Chesapeake Bay is not just a story about good food, rambling hotels and grand soirées; it is a story about leadership. The vision of people like Marshall Parks, Joseph Segar, Harrison Phoebus, John Chamberlin, Frank Darling and L.U. Noland transformed this land spit into a major resort. These businessmen recognized tourism's economic power. They knew that Old Point Comfort had the transportation links and natural attributes to become a vibrant source of revenue for themselves and their community. Without their foresight, there would not be a story to tell.

I am indebted to so many people for helping me create this Old Point Comfort resort book. First, I must thank my coauthor, Julia Steere Clevenger. We worked on this project, "amongst so many others," for eighteen months. Julia shaved away my extra words as she typed and edited the text. Miss Clevenger also prepared the recipe appendix, which provides a tasty glimpse into the food ways of this grand resort. Next, I must thank J. Michael Moore, Ashley Whitehead and Sara Johnston for their work researching, securing and preparing all of the images for this volume. Michael Cobb of the Hampton History Museum, Dave Johnson of the Casemate Museum and my son, John Moran Quarstein, must be thanked for providing the prints, paintings and photographs that appear in this volume. Michael Moore, who has assisted with all of my previous books, also helped to edit the text. My friend Julie Murphy served as another reader and editor. In addition to all of this technical support, many others provided me with their remembrances, which I was able to intertwine into the text. Betty Harper Wyatt, Gwen Cummings, Ross Kearney, Jim and Ann Tormey and Bob Allsbrook are just a few of the people who took the time to share their memories. I could not conclude these acknowledgements without lauding Wendy Drucker, John Munick and other members of the Drucker & Falk team who established a new vision for Old Point Comfort's last hotel. Their reuse concept and tremendous investment revitalized The Chamberlin, enabling it to continue towering over the Hampton Roads Harbor entrance as a symbol of Old Point Comfort's resort heritage.

Finally, I must thank my grandfather, John Lusk Kronau, for insisting on taking me on an Old Bay Line steamer and hosting me at The Chamberlin in 1960. He introduced me to the spoon bread that left me intrigued with the Old Point Comfort resort heritage.

INTRODUCTION

J ust over a century ago, Old Point Comfort was one of America's most popular vacation resorts. Thousands came weekly by steamboat and train. They found it fashionable to promenade along the Hampton Roads shoreline to witness military ceremonies at Fort Monroe. There were pavilions for dancing and special baths for the infirm. City dwellers found the sea air refreshing and the harbor scene romantic.

In 1900, there were two major hotels side by side between Fort Monroe's parapets and the Hampton Roads Harbor. The senior was the Hygeia, named for the Greek goddess of health, and the newer was The Chamberlin. Another hotel, the Sherwood Inn, was located near the fort's main gate next to St. Mary's Star of the Sea Catholic Church. Even though more than two thousand rooms were available in Old Point Comfort's hotels, the resort's popularity prompted more hotels to be built in the towns of Phoebus, Buckroe Beach and Grandview.

The Hygeia that stood in 1900 was the second hotel by that name at Old Point Comfort. The original Hygeia opened in 1822. The hotel quickly gained popularity, and by the 1840s, it was considered "large and commodious." It was torn down during the Civil War, however, and a new hotel was built next to the Old Point Wharf during the postwar era. Harrison Phoebus transformed the "new" Hygeia into one of the best-known hotels in the nation.

The new Hygeia's success brought competition in the guise of the Chamberlin Hotel. John Chamberlin, a famous restaurateur and gambler, began building his hotel in 1890. He ran out of money, and the work was

Old Point Comfort Wharf, circa 1958. *Courtesy of the Casemate Museum.*

The Chamberlin during restoration, 2008. *Courtesy of Drucker & Falk.*

finished by a corporation that kept the name Chamberlin. When it opened in 1896, it was the first hotel in the United States to be entirely illuminated by electric lights.

Meanwhile, the Hygeia faded and was torn down in 1903. The Chamberlin operated as a five-star hotel from the day its doors opened until it burned to the ground during a ferocious blaze in 1920. No lives were lost. It was replaced in 1928 by the brick Chamberlin.

During the 1920s and 1930s, The Chamberlin carried on the Old Point Comfort hospitality traditions. However, after World War II, the vacation needs of the American public changed. Eventually, the grand hotel fell into disrepair and was closed to the public in 2003. Acquired by Drucker & Falk, this National Register of Historic Places property was given new life when it was rehabilitated as a magnificent adult community. The Chamberlin's grand traditions of luxury, relaxed elegance, sense of place, stunning architecture, historical setting and spectacular panoramic views of the Chesapeake Bay and Hampton Roads have all been recaptured.

The Chamberlin still stands today as an elegant landmark welcoming ships into Hampton Roads Harbor. Its restoration offers a preview of how Fort Monroe will be transformed when the U.S. Army leaves the fort in 2011. The Old Point Comfort traditions of hospitality, health and holidays will certainly continue with The Chamberlin standing tall as a beacon of historic preservation and tourism.

Chapter 1
OLD POINT COMFORT

O ld Point Comfort is a land spit at the entrance to Hampton Roads. The point is located eighteen miles from the Chesapeake Capes. Originally called Cape Comfort by the English colonists in 1607, it quickly became known as Point Comfort. By the early eighteenth century, "old" was added to the point's name. The land spit is surrounded on three sides by water: the Chesapeake Bay, Hampton Roads and Mill Creek.

Captain John Smith called this land spit an "isle fit for a Castle." Old Point Comfort was first fortified in October 1609, when the Virginia colonists constructed Fort Algernourne. The fort burned down in 1612, and new forts were rebuilt to guard the entrance to the Virginia colony.

All ships entering the colony were required to stop at Old Point Comfort to pay "castle duties." Hence, the first Africans arriving in Virginia came first to Old Point Comfort in 1619.

The forts constructed on the point often fell into disrepair. By the time of the Second Anglo-Dutch Naval War, the Point Comfort fortifications were considered "useless." Colonel Miles Cary attempted to block a Dutch raid into Hampton Roads in 1667. Cary was mortally wounded, and the Point Comfort garrison was removed a few miles away to Jamestown.

Another fort was built following this devastating Dutch attack on the colony's tobacco fleet. Before the fort could be completed by Colonel Leonard Yeo, he reported that "the most Dreadful Hurry Cane that ever the colony groaned under" lashed Point Comfort. The storm lasted twenty-four hours. According to Yeo:

Captain John Smith. *Courtesy of the Hampton History Museum.*

The waves carried all the foundation of the fort at Point Comfort into the River and most of Timber which was very chargeably brought hither to perfect it. Had it been finished a garrison in it, they had been stormed by such an enemy as noe power by Gods can restrain and in all likelyhood drowned.

King Charles II sent an autographed letter to "his well beloved Governor of Virginia" and assigned a new commander, Thomas Beale, to "Castle Comfort." The fort probably followed General Assembly guidelines, having "eight great guns at the least, the walls ten foote thick at least." Despite this effort, Hampton Roads remained defenseless, enabling the Dutch to raid the harbor again in 1673 during the Third Anglo-Dutch Naval War.

Even though Old Point Comfort was reported to have mounted a battery containing seventy guns in 1711, a more permanent fortification was needed. The last fortification built during the colonial era was Fort George. This fort was constructed in 1728 and was considered so strong that "no ship could pass it without running great risk." Unfortunately, Fort George was destroyed by a hurricane in 1749 and was never rebuilt. Lieutenant General Earl Charles Cornwallis rejected Old Point Comfort as being "poorly situated for defense" and moved his army to Yorktown in 1781. The French briefly occupied the point during the Yorktown siege.

Old Point Comfort was abandoned and left vacant when the siege ended. When the Napoleonic Wars erupted in Europe, Congress was pressured to secure funds to create a coastal defense system. After many delays, a recommendation was made and money was appropriated to fortify Old Point Comfort. Before any work could begin, however, Thomas Jefferson assumed office as president. Jefferson, believing that coastal defenses were too costly, canceled the

An old map of the Chesapeake Bay region. *Courtesy of the Hampton History Museum.*

appropriation. The only local public works project that he approved was the construction of the Old Point Comfort Lighthouse in 1802.

The British invasion of the Chesapeake Bay during the War of 1812 changed everything. In June 1813, a British fleet entered the unprotected mouth of Hampton Roads. Although defeated at Craney Island on June 22, 1813, the British turned and sacked the town of Hampton three days later. The British continued their rampage throughout the Chesapeake region and burned Washington, D.C., in August 1814. The War of 1812 clearly indicated the need for a more effective defensive system against naval attack on the nation's harbors and coastal cities. When an 1817 U.S. Navy report called for the establishment of a major naval depot in the Hampton Roads region, Brigadier General Simon Bernard of the U.S. Army Coastal Defense Board recommended that Old Point Comfort be immediately fortified.

On April 21, 1817, Colonel Walter K. Armistead was ordered to Old Point Comfort to begin collecting material for the fort's construction. Lieutenant James Maurice, Armistead's assistant and the project's superintending engineer, ordered stone and acted "to employ a good wharf builder [to] extend and complete the wharf at Old Point Comfort, sufficiently large and substantial to allow there vessels to come alongside and unload at the same time." The fort's construction began in earnest in 1819.

Fort Monroe, named for eighth U.S. president James Monroe, would become the largest moat-encircled masonry fortification in the United States. The fort covered sixty-three acres, and the circumference of its walls was 1.3 miles in length. The 8-foot-deep moat, fed by sluice gates drawing water from Mill Creek, varied in width from 60 feet at the East Gate to 150 feet at the Main Sally Port. The fort's irregular plan featured seven fronts with seven large bastions. Fort Monroe was designed to mount 412 guns with a wartime garrison of 2,625 officers and men. The fort was officially completed in 1834.

The fort on Old Point Comfort quickly became one of the most important military installations in the South. Brevet Brigadier General Abraham Eustis established the Artillery School of Practice at the fort in 1824. However, the fort's location overlooking Hampton Roads made Fort Monroe a perfect assembly, training and embarkation site for troops mustered to serve in the Seminole War, Nat Turner's Rebellion, the Black Hawk War and the Mexican War. Many officers destined to gain acclaim during the Civil War served at Fort Monroe during the antebellum era. Robert E. Lee supervised the construction of the fort's moat in the 1830s, and his eldest son, George Washington Custis Lee, was born at Fort Monroe in 1831. Men like Joseph Eggleston Johnson, Jubal Anderson Early, John Bankhead Magruder, John A. Dix and Robert Anderson were among the many future Civil War leaders to pass through the fort's sally ports.

Chapter 2

IN HER SEPULCHER
DOWN BY THE SEA

The initial construction of Fort Monroe was a huge undertaking. Slaves and military convicts served as construction laborers. Despite the use of these workers, paid contractors were needed to provide skilled labor. Captain Mann P. Lomax noted the disarray caused by construction and the lack of adequate quarters. This situation was resolved in 1821 when Colonel Charles Gratiot gave permission to William Armistead, superintending engineer of Fort Monroe, and Marshall Parks, a local property owner and design engineer of the Dismal Swamp Canal, "to build accommodations for the engineers and construction workers outside the perimeters of the new moated fort."

By 1822, this establishment, named the Hygeia Hotel in honor of the Greek goddess of health, consisted of "one large room used for a parlor and dining room with four chambers on each side," according to an early advertisement. Williams H. Hawkins, formerly of the Eagle Tavern in Richmond, was the first manager of the Hygeia. Hawkins also welcomed the hotel's first notable guest, Kentucky politician Henry Clay.

Clay, "one of the Speakers of the House," was aboard the steamer *Norfolk* en route to Baltimore when it landed passengers on February 20, 1822, during "thick weather" and a snow storm. It was said that Clay and his companions had not worried about the storm but had feared the interruption of their card game.

Francis Taylor assumed management of the hotel in 1826 and announced that the Hygeia was "ready to accommodate 100 persons." Adjacent to the

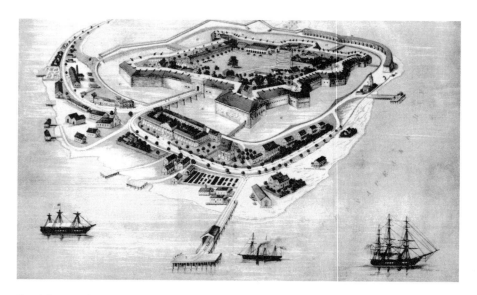

Fort Monroe. *Courtesy of John Moran Quarstein.*

main hotel building, Taylor advertised that there was a separate "house with four apartments for those who prefer warm bathing to cold." Taylor promoted the Hygeia, offering luxurious meals featuring "oysters, delicate fish, choice meats, and savory vegetables."

Sometime prior to 1830, Marshall Parks Sr. moved his family from Norfolk to Old Point Comfort. He took over from Taylor direct management of the hotel. His assumption of proprietorship coincided with President Andrew Jackson's use of Fort Calhoun on the Rip Raps Shoal as a presidential retreat. Jackson first visited Fort Monroe on July 9, 1829. The next day, Jackson, accompanied by several politicians and generals, including Secretary of War John H. Eaton and Brigadier General Simon Bernard, toured the Hampton Roads region. On his return from an inspection of Gosport Navy Yard, the president visited the Rip Raps Shoal to review progress on Fort Calhoun. Fort Calhoun, named for Jackson's vice president John C. Calhoun, was Fort Monroe's companion fortification. Jackson was impressed with the little island. He returned to the Rip Raps for ten days of rest during the Peggy Eaton controversy in August. Jackson was in poor health and spent his time bathing in the sea.

The president returned again in 1831, 1833, 1834 and 1835. His hotel at the Rip Raps was a delightful summer residence, one newspaper noted, "freely

President Andrew Jackson. *Courtesy of the Casemate Museum.*

inviting the breeze over the waters from every point of the compass, and with the polite and attentive host of the Hygeia, Mr. Marshall Parks, to cater for his table, he cannot be otherwise than 'comfortable.'"

During Jackson's last vacation on the Rip Raps, he was accompanied by a large group of friends and relatives. He often combined business with pleasure. On July 14, 1835, the president went to Fort Monroe to review the troops and witness a target firing by the thirty-two-pounder guns. Parks organized a boat to bring one hundred spectators from Norfolk to witness the event, but as a Norfolk Argus reporter noted:

> They were cruelly disappointed; the review was over two hours before they arrived and the target could not be adjusted in the desired position... in consequence of a strong breeze and high swell. But they saw the President...partook of the good cheer of the Hygeia, and came home tolerably reconciled.

The Hygeia's popularity increased during this era due to the imprisonment of Black Hawk and several of his leading men at Fort Monroe. News of Black Hawk's impending incarceration in Hampton Roads following the Black Hawk War prompted the *Norfolk Herald* to proclaim that the Indians would be "objects of much curiosity at Old Point Comfort." The editor advised Marshall Parks that unless he expanded "his already extensive establishment...he will very probably be at a loss for room to accommodate the visitors who will crowd upon him to see those 'Lions of the West.'"

A view of Fort Monroe's east gate. *Courtesy of John Moran Quarstein.*

Black Hawk and his fellow chieftains, Whirling Thunder and the Prophet, arrived at the Old Point Comfort Wharf aboard the steamer *Patrick Henry* on May 1, 1833. The Indian chieftain had a very lenient imprisonment and was free to move about the fort at ease. According to a newspaper reporter, Black Hawk and his men were "beset by visitors who crowded to see them from all quarters." Parks organized steamboat excursions to bring people to Old Point Comfort just for this purpose. Noted artists such as Robert M. Sulley and John Wesley Jarvis traveled to the Hygeia and painted portraits of Black Hawk. Black Hawk left Fort Monroe on June 4, 1833, to return to his people.

Marshall Parks had already recognized Old Point Comfort's future as a resort. He engaged Captain Andrew Talcott, an 1818 graduate of West Point and Fort Monroe's supervising engineer, to design an expansion. Talcott's "Plan of the Hygeia Hotel with the Projected Improvements" shows the Hygeia "Hotel Proper," with ancillary buildings laid out in an oblique triangular shape. A storehouse, kitchen, private room, dining room and "Ladies Drawing Room" were attached to the west wing. Other outbuildings at the rear of the hotel included two wash houses, a barbershop, a water bathhouse, a circular icehouse, a ten-pin bowling alley and three cisterns. The Hygeia Hotel underwent a substantial $1,700 improvement in 1837.

Marshall Parks also realized the importance of connecting Old Point Comfort with the major cities of the East and South. The James River Steamboat Company of Richmond, Virginia, with Marshall Parks as agent, was incorporated by an act of the Virginia Assembly on February 3, 1833, for the purpose of operating a steamer between Richmond and Norfolk. Steamship lines were already moving people and products up and down the Chesapeake by this time. The Baltimore Steam Packet Company offered the first steamer service on the bay in 1813. This company evolved into the Maryland & Virginia Steam Boat Company, which offered connections between Baltimore and Norfolk, as well as landings in towns throughout the Chesapeake region. The financial panic of 1837 forced this company into bankruptcy. It was then reorganized in 1840 as the Old Bay Line. A Mr. Smith recorded his arrival in Hampton Roads aboard the steamer *Georgia*:

> *The first gray streaks of approaching dawn found her skirting a fleet of fishermen in sailing canoes outward bound for the day's work on York Spit Shoals. She plowed steadily onward to meet short choppy seas washing over the Horseshoe, as the ebb tide ran counter to the gentle Sou-wester sweeping off the land. Soon she rounded Thimble Shoals and made her*

This famous lithograph by E. Sachse of Baltimore entitled "Fortress Monroe, Old Point Comfort and Hygeia Hotel, VA" depicts the Old Bay Line steamer *Adelaide* in the foreground. *Courtesy of John Moran Quarstein.*

way westward toward the mouth of Hampton Roads. The dock at Old Point Comfort lying below the guns of recently completed Fortress Monroe awaited and already some sleepy-eyed passengers who were getting off to stay at the Hygeia Hotel for the "bathing season" at the new resort were about on deck.

The *Georgia*, like other Old Bay Line steamers, would deposit passengers in Norfolk where they could take rail lines to the interior or board Atlantic Line boats to Charleston and other southern towns. The Old Bay Line would become the main line serving Old Point Comfort from Baltimore.

Marshall Parks Sr. died in 1840. In 1843, John S. Moody mortgaged the hotel and its fixtures and furnishings, valued at $2,000, with local businessmen Joseph Segar of Hampton and William Tazewell of Norfolk. The hotel inventory included:

38 double mattresses, 42 single mattresses,
30 featherbeds, 35 double bedsteads,
28 single bedsteads, 101 pillows, 78 bolsters,
132 linen sheets, 60 cotton sheets,
96 counter paines, 108 linen pillow cases,
26 cotton pillowcases, 244 chairs, 40 looking glasses,
40 pine tables, 20 mahogany tables, 10 fire sets, 8 mahogany wash stands,
52 pine wash stands, 100 window curtains, 12 worsted carpets,
100 pitchers, 100 linen & diaper towels, 480 plates, 60 dishes,
12 sets casters, 120 pieces china, 100 pieces glassware,
144 German silver spoons, 144 German silver teaspoons,
4 mahogany sofas, 40 sugar dishes, 100 salt cellars, 10 tablecloths,
4 single tablecloths, 8 mahogany bureaus, 4 pine bureaus,
1 billiard table

Additional improvements to the Hygeia Hotel were approved by the U.S. Army in 1844. The project, underwritten by John Moody, attached the east wing to the main hotel, incorporating a new dining room in the east wing and a kitchen in the "old back building" of the east wing.

In 1845, John Moody transferred the hotel ownership to James French. In 1850, French acquired two tracts of land and shoreline in Elizabeth City County known as "The Fishery" and "The Beach." French began making "preliminary arrangements…for the erection of an extensive hotel on the beach, not far from the fortress at Old Point, to be called the Virginia Ocean

In Her Sepulcher Down By the Sea

The original Hygeia Hotel. *Courtesy of the Casemate Museum.*

House." Before French could enact his plans, however, he sold the Hygeia in 1854 to Caleb C. Willard in partnership with Joseph Eggleston Segar. Willard, a Vermont native, also owned Willard's Hotel in Washington, D.C. Segar, an Elizabeth City County resident, was one of Hampton's leading attorneys, owned the "Roseland" Farm and served in the Virginia House of Delegates.

During the 1840s and 1850s, Old Point Comfort became the most fashionable resort in the South. As one writer commented:

> *At Old Point there is a splendid hotel, kept in excellent style; the tables, during the summer months, are plentifully supplied with the choicest viands, among which may be named the best of fish and oysters, which, with the superior facilities for sea-bathing and the delightful ocean breezes, the novelties and attractions connected with the fort, the convenient distance to Norfolk, Richmond, Washington, Baltimore, etc., unite to concentrate a large number of visitors there during the summer season in search of pleasure, and for the purpose of recruiting impaired health. Detached from the building, are extensive billiard saloons, bowling alleys, and pistol galleries, for exercise and amusement, and commodious bathing-houses; the groves of trees in front and rear of the house, afford an abundance of shade.*

Visitors enjoyed the waters and sea breezes, as well as entertainment provided by Fort Monroe's band and evening parades. These attributes attracted some of the leading citizens of the South.

Peninsula native John Tyler used Old Point Comfort as his presidential retreat. When Tyler's first wife, Letita Christian Tyler, died, the president sought the seclusion of the Rip Raps. During his several months' stay, he often

President John Tyler. *Courtesy of John Moran Quarstein.*

Julia Gardiner Tyler. *Courtesy of the Casemate Museum.*

dined at the Hygeia. On September 14, 1843, the president invited all of the officers of the garrison to dine with him at the Hygeia Hotel—and a right merry and pleasant party it was. The whole party adjourned to the ten-pin alley, where the president headed one side of the match game and Colonel John Walbach, the commander of the garrison, led the other. The president's side won the first game, and there was a tie in the second, which had to be decided by the president and Colonel Walbach each throwing a spare ball. Tyler knocked down eight pins and, turning to Colonel Walbach, remarked, "So distinguished a soldier as you might not to be beaten. I command you to beat this game. You have never disobeyed an order." The veteran (Walbach was seventy-eight at the time) replied, "I will endeavor, Mr. President, to do it." But he only knocked down five pins.

Tyler returned on July 4, 1844, when he married Julia Gardiner. They spent their month-long honeymoon at Old Point Comfort. The first two days of their stay were filled with social activities, concluding with all of the fort's officers marching as a group to pay their respects to the president and his bride. The Tylers returned to Old Point Comfort in June 1845 to celebrate their first anniversary at the Hygeia. In addition to the social activities, a hurricane struck, causing great commotion. As the storm ripped the roof off the hotel, Mrs. Tyler calmly rescued her canary.

Fort Monroe's garrison played a major role in the Hygeia's success. The pageantry of parades, theatrical exhibitions by soldiers and cannon drills offered enjoyments that few resorts could match.

Among the illustrious visitors to Old Point Comfort was Edgar Allan Poe. Poe was no stranger to the Hygeia. On December 20, 1828, Private E.A. Perry reported for duty at Fort Monroe. Perry was Poe's alias, which he used upon enlisting following his dismissal from the University of Virginia. Poe was promoted to sergeant major on January 1, 1829, and soon revealed his true identity and literary skills to his commanding officer, Lieutenant Joshua Howard. Poe, with Howard's assistance, was eventually able to secure his discharge by hiring a substitute. Poe left Fort Monroe on April 22, 1829, and entered the United States Military Academy, where he served until his dismissal on March 6, 1831.

Poe returned to Old Point Comfort two weeks before his death. He had been in Norfolk lecturing to raise funds in order to start his magazine, the *Stylus*. His topic was based on his essay "The Poetic Principle," in which he articulated that the business of poetry is to express the human aspiration for the beautiful. Since Poe believed that music is the medium in which beauty can be most nearly attained, he put forth the thought that the more poetry approaches true music the better it must be. His lecture was a success. Afterward, he took a steamer to Old Point Comfort and stayed at the Hygeia. On the evening of September 17, 1849, after dinner, Poe presented his last public reading of his poetry. He recited several of his works on the Hygeia's veranda, concluding with "Ulalume":

> *The skies they were ashen and sober;*
> *The leaves they were crisped and sere—*
> *The leaves they were withering and sere:*
> *It was night in the lonesome October*
> *Of my most immemorial year;*
> *It was hard by the dim lake of Auber,*
> *In the misty mid region of Weir—*
> *It was down by the dank turn of Auber,*
> *In the ghoul-haunted woodland of Weir.*

The next day, Poe took a steamer to Richmond; he died a few weeks later in Baltimore, Maryland. One poem was found amongst his papers

Edgar Allan Poe. *Courtesy of the Casemate Museum.*

following his death. "Annabelle Lee" is rumored to have been partially written while Poe was at the Hygeia and had also been recited during his September 17 performance. The final verse projects a visual connection with Old Point Comfort:

> *For the moon never beams, without bringing me dreams*
> *Of the beautiful Annabel Lee;*
> *And the stars never rise, but I feel the bright eyes*
> *   Of the beautiful Annabel Lee;*
> *And so, all the night-tide, I lie down by the side*
> *Of my darling,—my darling,—my life and my bride,*
> *   In her sepulcher there by the sea,*
> *   In her tomb by the sounding sea.*

The Hygeia had become so well known as a fashionable resort that it was used as the stage for a wide variety of fictional novels and magazine articles. One such story that appeared in *Graham's American Monthly Magazine of Literature and Fashion* projects a visual connection with Old Point Comfort:

> *What a glorious night! How dazzling look the shining sand, the glistening water, in the moon's mellow rays which fall now so brightly upon them, and bathing in its effulgence these two youthful figures who are pacing to and fro and the ramparts o Fortress Monroe, nearest the bay…*

In Her Sepulcher Down By the Sea

Vainly had he sought the interview during the day, but he could only see her as the centre of an admiring circle, for Edith was decidedly the "star of beauty" and the "belle" amid many who thronged the crowded salons of the Hygeia Hotel.

The Hygeia was indeed an elegant place. The building rambled along the western moat from the Main Sally Port to the First Bastion. The building had a Greek revival–style hipped roof with a low pitch. Doric columns supported the front porch and side verandas, topped with an emphasized wide band of trim that represented the classical en tablature and was divided into two parts: the frieze above and architecture below. The Hygeia had a dominant central porch extending to the building's full height. The wings had a colonnaded porch covering the full width and height of the façade.

Few descriptions of the building's interior remain other than the following comments by Edith Morton:

Have you ever been at Old Point Comfort? If you have 'tis needless for me to attempt to describe that spacious saloon, With corridors on each side—large enough to contain with ease at least five Hundred…what a coup d'ail [sic] struck on party as they entered the west door from the piazza. No garden ever gleamed more brightly with clustering flowers and mirrors reflecting its extensive range…making it look larger and better filled.

While socializing and romance often mingled with martial music and parade, it was the fresh and cooling sea breezes that made the Hygeia a success. After all, the hotel was named for the Greek goddess of health and accordingly was promoted as a health resort. Joseph Segar was the Hygeia's part owner and proprietor during the 1850s. Segar advertised that he was the hotel's sole owner in 1857 and promised to make the Hygeia the "most delightful Summer Resort…of all the sunny South." He purchased advertisements in publications such as the *American Farmer*:

For health, no mountain retreat can be safer, at any season of the year. It is exempt from disease in August and September and October, as in April, May or June. Indeed, the first three are infinitely the most pleasant of the season. The weather is milder, the sea breeze balmier, and the luxuries of the salt water, are to be had of finer quality, and in greater profusion. There is no more inviting spot on the whole Atlantic Seaboard. It is strictly true of it, what the Poet hath said: "Oh! If there be an Elysium on earth, it is this, it is this!"

Numerous testimonials from doctors were used to promote Old Point Comfort's healthy conditions. Fort Monroe's post surgeon, Dr. N.S. Jarvis, noted that after serving three years at the fort, it enabled him to attest to the site's "well known salubrity, and the reputation it has heretofore enjoyed in its exemption from the ordinary forms of disease, especially those of a malarial or febrile nature."

Dr. William Semple of Hampton stated that there was less sickness at Fort Monroe than at any other military post in the Union. He added:

> *Visitors at Old Point are as perfectly safe, at any season, from intermittent and remittent fever, as they would be in any mountain region. Patients suffering in such regions from bronchial affections particularly asthma, are uniformly benefitted by a visit to Old Point.*

Other medical men wrote of the "hygeaic conditions" and noted that "no climate can be purer or more delightful, or healthier." All commented that they "did not remember a case of bilious fever" originating at Old Point Comfort and joined in their praises of these breezes. Segar was striving to compete with spas such as White Sulphur Springs, Newport and Saratoga. The Honorable A. Dudley Mann, editor of *Debow's Review and Industrial Resources*, advised Segar:

> *Having just enjoyed the invigorating bath at this favorite resort for the sixty-first and last time during the present season, I shall proceed homeward this afternoon in as perfect health as ever mortal enjoyed. I have been for the last fifteen years an occasional visitor at the more distinguished watering places in Europe, and prior to my going abroad I repeatedly sojourned for a week or two in mid-summer at Newport, Nahant, and Saratoga; but I never quitted the sea-side or the mineral springs so reluctantly as I quit this time-honored historical spot—the virtues of whose baths and general atmosphere have endeared me by new, indissoluble bonds.*

The Hygeia welcomed over five thousand guests in the 1858 season, all of whom were seeking relief from the heat, as well as the freshness provided by the gentle yet invigorating sea breezes of Old Point Comfort.

The Hygeia's owners constantly sought ways to enhance visitation. A grand opportunity arose in the summer of 1860, when Old Point Comfort played host to the largest ship built up to that time. Known as the *Great Eastern*, it was five times the size of any ship then afloat, and its size would

Vessels at anchor at Hampton Roads. *Courtesy of the Casemate Museum.*

The Army of the Potomac passing the Hygeia Hotel, 1862. *Courtesy of the Casemate Museum.*

not be surpassed until the *Lusitania* was built in 1906. The *Great Eastern* was propelled by screw propeller, paddle wheels and sails. This iron-hull ship was capable of carrying four thousand passengers and was 679.6 feet in length. It was considered "the first wonder."

In May 1860, the *Great Eastern* went on its maiden voyage, docking in New York. The owners of the Old Bay Line convinced the ship's owner (with an added bonus of one thousand tons of coal) to make a special cruise to the Chesapeake. Only one hundred customers paid to enjoy the trip to Hampton Roads. The ship arrived at Old Point Comfort on August 3. Before the *Great Eastern* left for Annapolis on August 5, ten thousand visitors went to Old Point Comfort to see for themselves that an iron ship of such proportions could float. The Hygeia offered a special dinner and other entertainment for the ship's officers. The *Great Eastern* left Old Point Comfort with a full complement of passengers and was followed by virtually every vessel that could float on the Chesapeake Bay.

All of the gaiety on Old Point Comfort came to an end when war erupted between the North and the South. Even though Virginia left the Union on April 17, 1861, Fort Monroe and Old Point Comfort remained under Federal control. The Hygeia was partially converted into a hospital, and another part was occupied by the provost guard. Nevertheless, the hotel still welcomed guests, a practice that disrupted military activities. Secretary of War Edwin Stanton telegraphed Fort Monroe's commander, Major General John Ellis Wool, on March 14, 1862:

> *It is represented that a large number of visitors for pleasure, dealers in trade, and other persons not in the public service, are now congregating at Fort Monroe, whose presence may embarrass the grave naval and military operations now in progress or in contemplation there. You are authorized, in your discretion, to require the immediate departure of all persons not in the service of the United States, whose presence may incommode operations and to exclude unauthorized persons from stopping or remaining there, until further notice. You will, from and after this date, exercise the most rigid discipline and police within the territory under your command.*

Since the original agreement that enabled the Hygeia to be built allowed the army to dictate the hotel's demolition in times of war, the Hygeia was ordered to be torn down on September 1, 1862. The building was demolished on December 1, 1862.

Chapter 3
ENTER HARRISON PHOEBUS

S hortly after the Hygeia Hotel's demolition, Caleb Willard secured authorization to construct a one-story restaurant near Baltimore Wharf. This "eating house" was approved to benefit "transient officers" arriving at Old Point Comfort, and it became known as the Hygeia Dining Saloon.

The Baltimore Wharf was a major improvement completed by the U.S. Army in 1862. The Engineer's Wharf (also referred to as the Lighthouse Wharf) could not handle the increased usage caused by the 1862 Peninsula Campaign. Merchant seaman John A. Henriques had already noted how busy the Engineer's Wharf was, recording in 1848 that the steamer *Curtis Peck* "stopped at Old Point Comfort and landed our passengers…There is one wharf at this place and on this were piled a vast quantity of munition[s] wagons and harnesses." The 1862 wharf was designed to accommodate several ships simultaneously. Located at the end of present-day Ingalls Road, it became known as the Baltimore Wharf because of its predominant use by Old Bay Line steamers.

Willard soon sold his interest in the Hygeia Dining Saloon, and the business eventually passed to Henry Clark. Clark received permission on June 25, 1868, to "enlarge the said hotel." He formed a partnership with John E. Wilson on March 14, 1872. The hotel, capable of accommodating five hundred guests, was noted as being substantially built and comfortably furnished with all the modern appointments. The new owners promoted the Hygeia as a year-round resort worthy of its beautiful and historical surroundings. Advertisements promoted the Hygeia as a resort for pleasure

The Hygeia Dining Saloon. *Courtesy of the Casemate Museum.*

seekers, invalids and tourists en route to points both north and south. Old Point Comfort's excellent water connections—the Old Dominion Steamship Company from New York, the Old Bay Line from Baltimore, the steamer *Lady of the Lake* from Washington, D.C., and the steamer *John Sylvester* from Richmond—all reinforced ease of access.

Despite all of its attributes, the second Hygeia failed. The property was assigned to Thomas Tabb, Harrison Phoebus and G.S. Griffith Jr. as trustees for the creditors. The hotel was then sold to Samuel M. Shoemaker. Shoemaker, one of the owners of the Adams Express Company, secured authorization by an act of Congress, passed on February 19, 1875, to enlarge the hotel and reaffirm the conditions of the joint resolution of June 1868. He quickly enlarged the facility; however, Shoemaker sold the property on July 10, 1876, to Harrison Phoebus.

Harrison Phoebus, who would dominate the growth of Old Point Comfort and the Mill Creek community's transformation for the next ten years, was born on an Eastern Shore farm near Princess Anne, Maryland, on November 1, 1840. His father died when Harrison was young, so he begun tonging oysters at age fifteen. By eighteen, he was hauling lumber to sawmills and building houses. His determination and dedication were evident. When the Civil War erupted, he served as a private in the Eighth Maryland (Union) from October 29, 1862, to August 3, 1863. In the spring of 1864, he joined the Eleventh Maryland Infantry (Union), serving as quartermaster sergeant until he was mustered out of service on October 1, 1864.

Enter Harrison Phoebus

The second Hygeia Hotel. *Courtesy of the Casemate Museum.*

Phoebus was then living in Baltimore and applied to work at the Adams Express Company. He was willing to do "anything from sweeping the floors to writing a letter." He was put to work on an express wagon, and he did so well that he was assigned additional duties. Phoebus was detailed to Point Lookout, Maryland, where a prisoner of war camp for captured Confederates was sited. When the war ended, he was eventually made the agent of the Adams Express Company at Old Point Comfort.

This assignment was perfect for the ambitious and energetic Phoebus. He quickly assumed other duties: agent for several steamship lines, postmaster, notary public and U.S. commissioner at Fort Monroe. He sold insurance and made wise real estate investments in the little village of Mill Creek. Harrison Phoebus's greatest opportunity came when he convinced Shoemaker, an official of the Adams Express Company, to acquire the Hygeia Hotel.

Phoebus knew that with effective management and promotion, the Hygeia could become a successful enterprise. "I will have the best hotel of its kind and I will let the public know" was his motto. He learned everything there was to know about the hotel industry by visiting other facilities, studying new equipment and learning about the public's needs. Filled with this knowledge, Phoebus delightfully transformed the Hygeia into one of the best-known hotels in the nation, welcoming visitors from throughout the world.

The Hygeia was continually enlarged and improved. The four-star hotel was constructed in the Second Empire style. While Victorian architectural styles often looked to the romantic past for inspiration, Second Empire was

Harrison Phoebus. *Courtesy of John Moran Quarstein.*

considered very modern, for it initiated the latest French building fashions. The distinctive roof was named for the seventeenth-century architect François Mansart. Its use was extensively revived in France during the Second Empire reign of Louis Napoleon, from which the style takes its name. The boxy roofline was considered particularly functional because it permitted a full upper story of usable attic space. Although Second Empire style was used for public buildings, the second Hygeia was the largest example in Hampton Roads.

By 1882, the Hygeia had been enlarged with extensions, wings and annexes and had reached the stateliness, beauty and dimensions of a palace. The Hygeia could accommodate one thousand guests. The grand hotel stretched seven hundred yards from the Baltimore Wharf eastward, almost reaching the Old Point Comfort Lighthouse. The entire water frontage was encircled by two wide porches (it was noted that the porches ran one and one-eighth miles and were often enclosed in glass during the winter). The Hygeia had a 7,000-square-foot dance pavilion, eleven spacious parlors and a half dozen private dining rooms. Its eight hundred bedchambers, most of them elegantly furnished, had electric bells, or speaking tubes, enabling the guests to communicate with the main office for services of every kind. There were electric lights everywhere, powered by the hotel's own "dynamos," as well as telephones, Otis hydraulic elevators and every appliance known to modern man. The main dining room was 150 by 60 feet, with a great domed roof, which was separated from the ladies' parlor by a glass partition. Both rooms had luxurious furnishings. The walls were wainscoted in polished cherry wherever they were not covered with massive mirrors. The dominant feature of these rooms was an immense triangular chimney with three open fires, where, according to *Harper's Weekly*:

> *Dowager and duchess confab with senator and savant; here the shy bride seeks shelter from too curious eyes; here the brilliant belle who foregoes*

The Hygeia Hotel
. . .OLD POINT COMFORT, VA. . .

The second Hygeia Hotel. *Courtesy of John Moran Quarstein.*

> *waltzing for a season, sways with the wave of a fan her too willing slaves;*
> *and here the veteran whist-player finds foe men worthy of his steel.*

Harper's noted that the main foyer with its office area was called "the most noted hotel room in America, if not in the world." Another correspondent remarked about the grand foyer:

> *Through its windows of cathedral glass there is a superb view enlivened by*
> *dancing sunbeams, and fleeting sails, and reflected by the great mirrors upon*
> *every hand. From the great tiled chimney-piece, two celebrated terra-cotta*
> *eagles look over the assembled multitude from all over the country.*

Harrison Phoebus had spared no expense creating his grand hotel. An estimated $300,000 of his own money was expended on this endeavor. The Hygeia was noted as being "the most costly building on the Atlantic Coast."

Harrison Phoebus was tireless in building the hotel and community. He lobbied Collis Potter Huntington to extend the C&O Railroad from Newport News into Elizabeth City County. Huntington agreed: Milepost 0 for the C&O was placed at the Old Point Comfort Station, not more than two hundred yards from the Baltimore Wharf and, of course, the Hygeia. This action greatly enhanced access to the resort. Old Point Comfort welcomed fifteen to twenty steamers daily (except Sunday). The new rail connection brought visitors swiftly and safely from the nation's interior to the grand hotel.

One of the Hygeia's verandas. *Courtesy of the Casemate Museum.*

Harrison Phoebus's Hygeia Hotel. *Courtesy of John Moran Quarstein.*

A view of the Hygeia from the water. *Courtesy of the Hampton History Museum.*

Travelers arrive at the Hygeia Hotel. *Courtesy of the Hampton History Museum.*

Phoebus had also invested heavily in the growing town of Chesapeake City, formerly the village of Mill Creek. Because of its proximity to the National Soldier's Home, the National Cemetery and Hampton Institute, a depot, named Phoebus, was built in Chesapeake City. Shortly thereafter, a new post office was built and named "the Phoebus PO." According to a newspaper report:

> *Mr. Legrand Donohue has received his commission as postmaster of the village. It was the first mail at the new office and addressed to Phoebus, Elizabeth City Co., VA. The office, like the C.O. [sic] depot, as Donohue noted took its name from the popular proprietor of the Hygeia Hotel at the Point. Mr. Phoebus, being recognized as the power behind the throne that builds up our town in business.*

Chesapeake City was growing quickly, with small hotels and saloons available for those who could not stay on Old Point Comfort but still wished to enjoy the resort's gaiety and sea breezes. In 1900, the community was incorporated as a town by the name of Phoebus.

The Hygeia brought Harrison Phoebus tremendous wealth, power and honor. In 1883, he acquired the famous White Sulphur Springs Hotel in Greenbrier County, West Virginia. Phoebus intended to improve the hotel to "render it more than ever the most delightful of America Spas. The management will be conducted on the same liberal principles which have contributed so largely to the success of the Hygeia." Harrison Phoebus had risen to success just like one of the heroes of a Horatio Alger book. He was described by one acquaintance in 1882 as

> *still a young man in appearance he is thick-set and fast developing into a rotundancy of Falstaffian proportions. His head is well shaped, his face round and covered [in a] thick beard and moustache; his eyes are his best feature and they are clear, searching and piercing. Indeed he is such a good fellow and bears such a resemblance to certain high cards in the pack that he goes entirely by the name of "King of Trumps."*

By early 1886, Phoebus had reached the height of his career. He had acquired the estate of Roseland on Strawberry Banks and had begun to build a manor house there when he died of heart disease on February 25. Harrison Phoebus was just forty-five years old, yet he left a powerful legacy that would influence his community for decades after his death.

Chapter 4

THE CHAMBERLIN

Harrison Phoebus was able to capitalize on Old Point Comfort's unique geographical situation. Just eighteen miles from the Virginia Capes and overlooking the lower Chesapeake Bay, the sea breezes gave fame to the Hygeia's claim as a health resort, while the waterways offered access to travelers from throughout the Atlantic Coast and Europe. Phoebus had welcomed such luminaries as David Kalakaua, the king of Hawaii, as well as socialites and business magnates in droves.

Here lov'd Hygeia holds her blissful seat
And smiles on all who seek her blessed retreat

Of course, Phoebus's success prompted others to strive to emulate, or at least share in, the resort's appeal. The first competitor was the Sherwood Inn. Dr. Robert Archer, formerly Fort Monroe's chief surgeon, built a cottage after he resigned from the U.S. Army in 1840. He had assumed the role of post sutler and located his home across Ingalls Road from the Main Sally Port. His home became an eating house and soon was welcoming overnight guests. Eventually, Mrs. S.F. Eaton acquired the Sherwood Inn in 1867. Mrs. Eaton continued to expand the property. By 1889, it was acquired by George Booker, who named it the Sherwood Inn after his family's plantation. The Sherwood Inn was promoted as being "delightful all the year...Cuisine Excellent." On the evening of December 22, 1896, the three upper stories of the inn were burned. The structure was quickly rebuilt and operated for the next twenty years as the New Sherwood.

The Sherwood Inn. *Courtesy of John Moran Quarstein.*

In the nearby town of Hampton, the Barnes Hotel was opened in the 1870s. While primarily catering to businessmen, the hotel was advertised as a "popular Summer Resort open all the year" with "all the Advantages of Old Point Comfort at Cheaper Rates." Another noted hostelry was the Augusta Hotel on East Queen Street. When the Barnes Hotel was demolished in 1902, the Augusta became Hampton's premiere hotel. The hotel's motto was "On the shore with open doors, prepared to shelter and feed the wayfarer and stranger." Chesapeake City, or Phoebus, as it would commonly be called at the turn of the century, also directly benefited from the Old Point Comfort resort.

By 1890, the town had at least eight hotels: the Elk's Retreat–Chesapeake Hotel, Clark's Palace, the Atlantic Garden Hotel, the Phoebus Club Hotel, Hotel Richelieu, Hotel Klondyke, Fuller's Hotel and Brightview Cottage. Brightview Cottage was sited on Mill's Creek. Since it had an outstanding view of Fort Monroe across Mill Creek, it primarily served military families and their guests. Brightview was an antebellum house that had been used as a convalescent hospital during the Civil War and was converted into a hotel in 1895. Clark's Hotel on Mallory Street, with its Richardson Romanesque motifs, was one of the most ornate buildings in Phoebus. Fuller's Hotel could accommodate 475 guests and feed more than 500. Fuller's was noted for providing the best meals on the peninsula and offered a wide range of "wetgoods" said to be "large, varied, and selected with sound judgment." Phoebus, according to the 1900 *Hill's Directory*, was home to fifty-two saloons.

One of Old Point Comfort's premier attractions was its beaches. From the Baltimore Wharf, a continuous white sand beach stretched to Factory Point at the entrance to the Back River. As sea bathing grew in popularity and rail connections reached Phoebus, this beach area offered a major opportunity to expand Elizabeth City County's tourism industry. In 1883, Mary Ann Dobbins Herbert acquired part of the Buckroe Plantation and opened a boardinghouse for summer guests. A bathhouse and dance pavilion were added shortly thereafter. Edward Chiles of Hampton built Buckroe's first public bathhouse a year later. Chiles transported his patrons to the beach in horse-drawn wagons. Buckroe's future as a resort seemed ensured when the Buckroe, Phoebus and Hampton Railway Company was formed. Captain Frank Darling organized the Newport News, Hampton and Old Point Railway Company by merging two existing firms. Darling then acquired the Buckroe, Phoebus and Hampton Railway Company. The old trolley service tracks were replaced with sixty-five-pound steel rails that allowed C&O excursion trains from Richmond to reach Buckroe during the summer months. Another bay-front hotel was built in 1890, a few miles from the Fox Hill community. The Grandview resort featured a dance pavilion. An attractive horse-drawn wagon drove guests from the Hampton and Phoebus depots, as well as the Old Point Comfort Wharf, to enjoy the beach at Grandview.

Guests on the beach at Old Point Comfort. *Courtesy of the Casemate Museum.*

J.S. Darling, Frank Darling's father, purchased land at Buckroe Beach and opened the Buckroe Beach Hotel on June 21, 1897. The hotel featured a large dance pavilion and was managed by Charles H. Hewins. The Buckroe Beach Hotel eventually became known as a family hotel, offering good accommodations and excellent food in a dignified atmosphere. Buckroe Beach continued to expand during the early twentieth century and became a popular middle-class retreat for Richmond residents. Buckroe had a bowling alley, a pool hall, a Ferris wheel, a penny arcade and other amusements.

Virginia's first beach resort for African Americans opened in 1898 between Buckroe Beach and Fort Monroe. Known as the Bayshore Hotel, it became a successful venture, welcoming blacks who used the C&O and trolley connections to enjoy the summer waterfront climate.

When Harrison Phoebus died, management of the Hygeia was assumed by F.N. Pike. Pike endeavored to operate the hotel with the same success that Phoebus had achieved. Pike advertised that people wishing to escape from the rigors of a northern winter could find no more agreeable southern resort than the Hygeia on Old Point Comfort. He promoted the Hygeia as a model hotel for people who were in search of health and recreation. The Hygeia appeared to offer everything that a traveler, invalid, socialite or bon vivant could desire. Pike maintained Phoebus's two missions: the social and the sanitary. The *Boston Saturday Evening Gazette* promoted the Old Point Comfort "climate…[as] delightful…absolutely free from malaria, and the air is balmy and full of life giving ozone…and the drainage and other sanitary arrangements are perfect." The sea breezes offered a refreshing respite from the summer's heat. The Hygeia sought to compete with spas like White Sulphur Springs and Saratoga Springs, therefore:

a complete set of baths, including the Turkish, Russian, Thermo, Electro, Magnetic, Mercurial, Sulphur and Vaporbaths have been introduced which combined with celebrated Hot Sea Baths, adds another and wonderful agent to the therapeutic advantages of the Hygeia, as beneficial as it is unique.

The verandas had glass enclosures that enabled the "most delicate invalid to enjoy the sunshine and fine waterview without the slightest exposure" during the winter months.

As a social gathering place, the Hygeia had few peers. Fort Monroe's proximity to the area prompted one writer to remark that it appeared that it was the "duty of a paternal government to place its military and naval stations close to the fashionable resorts." Fort Monroe was then considered

The Buckroe Beach Hotel, circa 1900. *Courtesy of the Hampton History Museum.*

The Bayshore Hotel, circa 1940. *Courtesy of the Hampton History Museum.*

The sea breezes at Old Point Comfort
were thought to promote health.
Courtesy of John Moran Quarstein.

one of the most historical places in America, just a few "minutes' walk and always open to visitors." A *Harper's Weekly* article in 1888 reflected:

Every room of this big wooden labyrinth has its drowsing occupant, and, sleeping or waking, there are more beauties in the corridors of the Hygeia or along the shaded walks within the fort than one can meet in a decade of travel...Perhaps the proximity of Fortress Monroe has not a little to do with the popularity of Old Point Comfort as a health resort. Day after day, in their dainty dresses, swarms of charming girls invade the fort, supervise the "mechanical maneuvers," criticize the battery drills, demoralize the "star gazers" (a detachment of student-officers who are almost daily at work inspecting the bores of their barbette guns, and making impressions of familiar old cracks and flaws that every class has stumbled over for years past), and only appearing conquered by circumstances when they suddenly find themselves in attendance at target practice and compelled to stand the roar and concussion of the big black boomers. Even around the hotel, the military air prevails. The Artillery Band comes in every day and plays in the salon adjourning the great dining room, and officers off duty dine with their friends, and point out historic spots in the neighborhood...and when sunset nears and the bugles blare the signal for parade, hundreds of gaily

An engraving from *Harper's Weekly* titled "Where Mars and Venus Collide," by E.G. Zogbaum. *Courtesy of John Moran Quarstein.*

dressed visitors stream across the moat and through the resounding postern and over the green carpet of the parade, where they make a picturesque group under the grove of oak trees; and then the band strikes up, and the troops march out and form line of battle, and there is a brief quarter-hour of music and martial pomp, and then the officers march up to the front, briefly salute their commander, and are swallowed up in the throng of civilians; and then twilight comes, and an adjournment to the hotel, and an evening devoted to more music and dancing, and the artillery uniforms are evidently as much at home in the salon as on the ramparts.

Left: An invitation to a Hygeia soirée. *Courtesy of the Hampton History Museum.*

Below: John F. Chamberlin. *Courtesy of the Casemate Museum.*

JOHN CHAMBERLIN.

Fort Monroe, while being the focal point of social interaction for the Hygeia's patrons, was not the only historical attraction. The nearby places of interest included Hampton, with its venerable St. John's Church; the beautiful Roadstead; the Hampton Normal and Agricultural Institute; the National Cemetery; and the Home for Disabled Soldiers. Leonard Sheetz's Hampton and Old Point Chariot Line provided transportation (at the cost of fifteen cents) between Hampton and the Baltimore Wharf on Old Point Comfort.

The Hygeia appeared to be the perfect resort. When the unsurpassed healthfulness and epicurean cuisine (embracing every delicacy of land and seafood) were coupled with Fort Monroe's charms, the Hygeia became one of America's greatest attractions. This situation was not overlooked by John F. Chamberlin.

Chamberlin was born in Lansingburg, New York, and got his start as a professional Mississippi riverboat gambler. After the Civil War, he went back East to run an exclusive gambling club at Long Branch, New Jersey. Chamberlin was "literally rolling in wealth" when the Panic of 1873 left him "dead broke." He then moved to Washington, D.C., where he used his influential gambling friends' connections to obtain the rights to run a restaurant at the House of Representatives. Known as Chamberlin's, the restaurant quickly became a gathering spot for politicians and wealthy capitalists. Chamberlin was recognized as a gourmet of rare distinction. The cuisine was excellent, and the restaurant earned a reputation for serving the best canvasback and terrapin soup in Washington. "No such place ever existed before, or will ever exist again," journalist Henry Watterson wrote of the restaurant. "It was the personality of John Chamberlin, pervasive yet invisible, exhaling a silent, welcoming radiance."

Chamberlin had long wished to establish a grand hotel that could provide a legacy for his family. He was able to utilize his connections to secure a joint resolution of Congress, approved on March 3, 1887, that authorized him to construct a hotel on Old Point Comfort. The only caveat was that he obtain the consent of the Commonwealth of Virginia. In 1890, the Old Point Comfort Hotel Company was incorporated.

Chamberlin hired John Smith Meyer, the architect of the Library of Congress, to design his grand hotel. While he was able to gain the financial backing of California senator George Hearst, Pennsylvania Railroad president A.J. Cassat and banking magnate J.P. Morgan, the project encountered problems due to a lack of funds. The Holtzclaw Brothers was the contractor and had recently completed the renovation of another Old

The Hotel Chamberlin.
Courtesy of the Casemate Museum.

Point Comfort hotel, the Sherwood Inn. The Chamberlin's groundbreaking occurred in July 1890; work progressed rapidly. The first projected completion date was March 1, 1891. Crews worked over the Thanksgiving holiday, and electric lights were installed so that construction could continue throughout the night. The hotel was still unfinished in 1891, when work was suspended. Work resumed a week later. Eventually, Chamberlin's company went into bankruptcy and the Holtzclaw Brothers suffered a loss. Nevertheless, Chamberlin was somehow able to bring the resources together and organized a grand opening of his magnificent hotel on April 4, 1896.

Visitors began arriving via a special C&O excursion train on the morning of April 4 to view the new hotel, which was promoted as being "among the largest and the most attractive of American watering place hostelries." Notable personages from New York, Philadelphia, Baltimore and Richmond joined a contingent of five hundred from Washington. A few of the most distinguished attendees included Postmaster General William Wilson, governor of Virginia Charles Triplett O'Ferrall, Secretary of the Navy Hilary Abner Herbert and U.S. Army commanding general Nelson A. Miles, along with numerous congressmen and senators. The U.S. Marine Band provided the entertainment. The U.S. Navy Atlantic Fleet White Squadron, consisting of the flagships *New York*, *Maine*, *Cincinnati*, *Raleigh*, *Columbia* and *Montgomery*, was stationed just off Old Point Comfort's Baltimore Wharf and offered tours to the fifteen hundred attendees. The opening ceremony was a splendid affair and concluded with the Marine Band playing "Auld Lang

Syne." Attendees sang along. At its close, three hearty cheers were given for John Chamberlin. A marvelous banquet and gala ball followed. All attendees were amazed at the hotel's furnishings, design and hospitality. The next day, Easter Sunday, featured special religious services in Fort Monroe's chapel and aboard the warships.

John Chamberlin died four months later, on August 22, 1896, of Bright's disease at the Grant Union Hotel in Saratoga Springs, New York. He was flat broke and left behind only his name, friends and debt. The grand hotel he created was his sole gift to posterity.

Chapter 5

WHERE MARS AND VENUS COLLIDE

The Hotel Chamberlin's opening presented an impressive site for travelers arriving at the Baltimore Wharf. Old Point Comfort was now truly a major resort, with two grand hotels positioned side by side along the waterfront. The Chamberlin was called the largest hotel in Virginia and cost an estimated $5 million to construct. The hotel was 754 feet long and had six stories containing 554 rooms and one thousand beds. Many of the rooms were rather lavish, "200…having private baths of handsome design into which may be turned hot or cold, fresh or salt water." Many rooms were available with private parlors, while others opened onto porticos. Every room offered a spectacular view. The hotel was basically surrounded on three sides by water, and the fourth side looked out at Fort Monroe. One of the hotel's brochures likens the experience with "the sensation of being at sea." The verandas and porches overlooked Hampton Roads. Glass inserts were designed to allow guests to enjoy these views during the colder months without blocking the fresh sea breezes during warmer months. The Chamberlin was planned as a year-round resort.

The large pavilion was actually built of iron and glass over the water. Its smoothly polished wooden floor was a perfect dancing space. During the summer, the glass was opened to enable the guests to enjoy the soothing sea breezes. The Palm Garden was considered one of the most pleasing features of the hotel. This space, the sun porch and the spacious balcony, with its handsome balustrade, were erected along the waterfront, adjacent to the pavilion, offering "every advantage of an ocean voyage without any of the

A glimpse at the interior of the Hotel Chamberlin. *Courtesy of the Hampton History Museum.*

An aerial view of The Chamberlin. *Courtesy of the Casemate Museum.*

inconvenience." The balcony was especially noted as being "perfect for out of door promenading."

Everything about the great hotel was impressive. The Chamberlin offered the most modern equipment, including electric lights powering the entire hotel. The public space was considered palatial. A guest was immediately impressed with the use of space in the main foyer. The general form of this "great room" was in the imprint of a Greek cross.

Everywhere was evidence of John Chamberlin's exquisite taste. He had the skill of a master hand in decorations, furnishings and finish. The main corridor was four hundred feet in length. Off this corridor was the main dining room. This high space had an elevated gallery, which afforded guests a fascinating view from above the main floor. At one end was a balcony, where the large orchestra was located during the entire dining hour. Nearby, off the main corridor, was an elaborately furnished ballroom with a spring floor of the finest quality and smoothness of finish. It was brilliantly lighted, and special attention was given to the room's acoustics and ventilation.

Just like the Hygeia, The Chamberlin was promoted as a health resort. Great awareness was given to the Hampton Roads region's location on the Gulf Stream. This circumstance, it was said, made the climate so equable and, at all times, beneficial. Old Point Comfort's pure saltwater air and breezes were strongly promoted as "life-giving." Advertisements clarified the point that the new hotel was not a sanitarium; rather, it existed to help patrons to "build up, to rest, and sleep…Everybody sleeps well here. The quiet and the salt laden air conquer insomnia. Sleepless nights are not at Old Point Comfort."

The Chamberlin offered spa-like benefits. The Hydrotherapeutic Department offered all sorts of medicinal baths, including Nauheim baths, continuous or massage baths and cabinet baths. The staff "especially recommend those baths in which the pure sea water is used" and added that the marked benefits would help "relieve numerous rheumatism, gout and kindred disorders." An added bonus was the hotel's Pompeian swimming pool. The saltwater pool was called "the most magnificent in America," radiant with sunlight in the day and brilliantly illuminated at night.

John Chamberlin's hotel was a brilliant addition to the Old Point Comfort scene. The hotel offered a variety of amusements, including sailing, tennis and dancing. The Chamberlin supported the opening of the Hampton Roads Golf Club in 1893. It was the first of its kind in Virginia. Golf's popularity prompted The Chamberlin to build its own course nearer to the hotel on the outskirts of Phoebus. A hunting lodge on a ten-thousand-acre

The Blue Parlor at the Hotel Chamberlin. *Courtesy of the Hampton History Museum.*

The Hotel Chamberlin. *Courtesy of the Casemate Museum.*

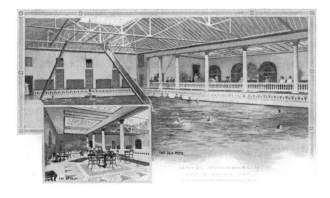

The Chamberlin's saltwater swimming pool. *Courtesy of the Hampton History Museum.*

The Chamberlin's hunting lodge on the Chickahominy River. *Courtesy of the Hampton History Museum.*

preserve was acquired on the Chickahominy River for duck hunting, and sports were also offered, with special hunting excursions to Cobb's Station on the Eastern Shore. Fishing opportunities in the bay, ocean and nearby rivers were readily available. One Old Point Comfort resort patron wrote to his friend Louise in 1899:

> *Have just returned from my daily fish and must answer your sweet letter. The day has been most delightful and 6 hours on the bay inhaling the bracing air from the sea makes me feel that life is worth living. Yesterday we caught 115 and today 251. What do you think of that.*

The Chamberlin was a complete resort, ready to cater to every recreational need of its sportsmen and patrons.

All the amenities of The Chamberlin made the Hygeia appear aged. The Hygeia had fallen into a slow decline since the death of Harrison Phoebus. Eventually, it was acquired by the Old Point Comfort Hotel Company. F.N. Pike was retained as manager, and the Hygeia continued its traditions: social grace, entertainment and health-giving baths. The Chamberlin was new and opulent; consequently, it became the main attraction. However, the New York, Washington and Virginia social sets continued to stay at the

The Chamberlin and the Hygeia, side by side. *Courtesy of John Moran Quarstein.*

Hygeia. Luminaries like the governor of Virginia, General Fitzhugh Lee, spent the season at the Hygeia in 1903. He was fortunate to have had this opportunity because the War Department ordered that the Hygeia and several other structures be razed. It appeared that the old hotel was in the way of military activity. The Chamberlin and the Sherwood Inn were excluded from this order. The Hygeia was given a brief reprieve and was not demolished until shortly after the Easter holiday in 1904. The Hygeia's grand pavilion remained, and it was used by the Coast Artillery Band until the structure's destruction during the devastating 1933 hurricane that ravaged Old Point Comfort.

With the Hygeia gone, The Chamberlin became the center of all social activities on Old Point Comfort. George Adams became the hotel's manager, and he promoted his property as the "Year-Round Resort of America." Adams confidently proclaimed that the "climate is unsurpassed. The Cuisine…perfect," and the "Historical Surroundings are absolutely unique." He expanded the active recreational opportunities, improved awareness of Old Point Comfort's transportation links and lauded his resort as being "the famous rendezvous of the Army, the Navy and Society" in Tidewater Virginia's colonial, naval and military heritage. These historical connections became especially important as the nation approached the 300th anniversary of the English colonists' arrival at Jamestown Island. The selection of Sewell's Point, directly across the harbor from Old Point Comfort in Norfolk, to host the 1907 Jamestown Expedition was considered a tremendous boon for Elizabeth City County and particularly for The

The Hygeia's grand pavilion. *Courtesy of the Casemate Museum.*

Chamberlin. Hotels throughout the county were refurbished and expanded; however, none could match the elegance, reputation or location of The Chamberlin. Plans were made for a great naval and marine exhibition in the waters of Hampton Roads.

Adams produced a booklet entitled *The Marvelous Diary of Captain John Smith, late President of His Majesties Colony of Virginia—Recently Discovered at Hotel Chamberlin Ould Poynt Comfort Virginia*. It was a fanciful tale of John Smith rediscovering the wonders of Virginia in 1907 via his sojourn at The Chamberlin. Delicate woodcut images were created to tell Smith's tale, as well as how he was mysteriously "transported" into the twentieth century to participate in the Jamestown Exposition. Of course, Smith offered a "Chamberlin" perspective of Virginia and in doing so promoted The Chamberlin's features, such as the Room of Palms, the Grand Hall, dining, what could be seen and enjoyed by touring Fort Monroe (he referred to it as Fort Algernourne), playing golf and duck hunting. His tale concluded with a farewell ghostly lament:

> *Alack. My dream is ended. I must this night set forth for the realm of spirits, which I have so long inhabited. Indeed, times be so changed that I am ill at ease in this new day; and so, farewell! The world hath indeed traveled far since I was of it. Jamestown is but a romantic memory; my deeds are legends; and with a sad heart I leave behind me the comforts*

A woodcut engraving for the Jamestown Exposition. *Courtesy of the Hampton History Museum.*

of Hotel Chamberlin. And while I may never again visit that "Point of Comfort" yet one comfort carry hence. With what wondrous tales may I not confuse the ears of such comrades of mine old days, as fare forth when the clocks give tongue to midnight! A worthy teller of travel tales I ever was; but by my troth, never until now had I such marvels to relate!

The high point of the Jamestown Exposition was the great naval rendezvous. The U.S. Atlantic Fleet arrived in Hampton Roads on April 15, 1907, and anchored near the Old Point Comfort Lighthouse. Soon, squadrons from other nations, including Great Britain, France, Germany, Italy and Chile, joined the American fleet. Over seventy-five warships were in position when the Jamestown Exposition opened on April 26, 1907. The combined fleets were a big attraction, as one popular song, "Uncle Sam's Big Navy," proclaimed:

> *Meet me on the war path at the Jamestown Fair*
> *Uncle Sam's big Navy and his soldier boys are there*
> *Everybody's merry and it's grand you'll all declare*
> *Meet me on the warpath at the Jamestown Fair*

The fleet, along with President Theodore Roosevelt's attendance opening the exposition, transformed the event, in one account, from "Jamestown to

A view from Fort Monroe at night. *Courtesy of John Moran Quarstein.*

jingoism," in the hope that "people from the North will come and bring their boodle." The Chamberlin sought to take advantage of all of these activities. Two ferries ran from Old Point Comfort through the assembled fleets and then on to Sewell's Point, where sightseers enjoyed the exhibits. Charles Herbert was one of many Jamestown Exposition attendees who stayed at The Chamberlin. He wrote to his friend Helen Emmart in Baltimore:

> *What a wonderful time we have enjoyed at Old Point. The hotel is exquisite and meals divine. Today is our second crossing of the harbor to reach the Jamestown Fair. We steam through the grand assembled fleets. Our new ships are big and powerful. I saw an old Monitor left over from the war. The tiny ship would be no match to our new battleships. Tomorrow, I will attend a Captain mess aboard the* Kentucky. *This occasion should be a fine finish to my historic travels.*

The Chamberlin built on the success it attained during the Jamestown Exposition and recognized that heritage tourism was a key visitor draw. During the following year, 1908, The Chamberlin advertised:

> *The Historic Surroundings are absolutely unique. Williamsburg, Jamestown, Yorktown, are right at hand. Fortress Monroe, with "all*

This page and next: 1. Ads featuring the first Chamberlin as a place where young ladies could enjoy "Both Arms of the Service," circa 1900. *Courtesy of the Hampton History Museum.*

2.

3. The restored Roof Garden, 2008. *Courtesy of Drucker & Falk.*

4. The restored and refurbished Chesapeake Dining Room, 2008. *Courtesy of Drucker & Falk.*

5. A military parade marching down Fenwick Road in front of The Chamberlin's main entrance, circa 1900. *Courtesy of John Moran Quarstein.*

6. The Chamberlin at night. This view highlights that The Chamberlin was the first hotel to boast electric lights in every room, circa 1900. *Courtesy of John Moran Quarstein.*

13169. Sherwood Inn, Old Point Comfort, Va.

7. The Sherwood Inn, circa 1900. *Courtesy of John Moran Quarstein.*

8. The "new" Chamberlin-Vanderbilt Hotel, 1928. *Courtesy of John Moran Quarstein.*

9. A night view of The Chamberlin-Vanderbilt Hotel, circa 1930. *Courtesy of John Moran Quarstein.*

10. A steamboat making an evening landing at Old Point Comfort Wharf, circa 1910. *Courtesy of John Moran Quarstein.*

The New Chamberlin Hotel, Old Point Comfort, Virginia

11. A bird's-eye view of The Chamberlin and Fort Monroe. Note the original cupolas, circa 1930. *Courtesy of John Moran Quarstein.*

12. The Chamberlin and Fort Monroe, circa 1970. *Courtesy of John Moran Quarstein.*

13. The outdoor pool with the Old Point Comfort Wharf in the background, circa 1940. *Courtesy of John Moran Quarstein.*

A booklet advertising The Chamberlin. *Courtesy of John Moran Quarstein.*

the pomp and circumstance of war" is our next door neighbor. Hampton Roads, the most magnificent marine panorama in the world, is immediately before us.

George Adams ran ads in elite magazines featuring a scene by Charles Dana Gibson. The image depicted a lovely young belle encountering two young officers. Entitled "Both Arms of the Service," it reinforced the pleasurable social life found at The Chamberlin.

The hotel became a magnet for young officers. Many lieutenants formed a mess at the hotel, and for $42.50 per month, they could have all the food they could eat. Every afternoon there was a full-dress parade on the fort's parade grounds. Many officers would then proceed to The Chamberlin for a tea dance. The hotel hostess often would introduce young ladies visiting The Chamberlin to these young officers. Reportedly, there was a room off the ballroom known as the "Padded Cell," complete with a round table and chairs where introductions and rendezvous could be made.

All of the gaiety ended with World War I. Fort Monroe was bustling with soldiers, and The Chamberlin was requisitioned, along with the Sherwood Inn, for officers' billets. Once the war was over, The Chamberlin was returned to the Old Point Comfort Hotel Corporation. Unfortunately, The Chamberlin was never able to return to its prewar glory. Tragedy struck at

Sailors performing a gun drill. *Courtesy of the Hampton History Museum.*

Where Mars and Venus Collide

Women pose for a photograph at Fort Monroe. *Courtesy of the Casemate Museum.*

An aerial view of The Chamberlin. *Courtesy of the Casemate Museum.*

The Chamberlin on fire. *Courtesy of the Casemate Museum.*

5:00 p.m. on March 7, 1920. A hotel staff member asked the guests for a fire extinguisher. A fire had started in the second-floor beauty shop caused by defective wiring. The building was not fireproof, and the blaze quickly spread out of control. Phoebus resident Sam Haywood recalled that it "was quite a fire. You could see it for miles around in Newport News, Chesapeake, and Norfolk." The intense heat sent flaming debris into the harbor and nearby buildings. Adams Express Co., John Kimberly's general store and two military classroom buildings were destroyed by the flames. Many of the fourteen hundred guests were taken in by army families whose quarters were nearby. Not a life was lost, even though the flames destroyed the hotel in three hours. The Chamberlin was a complete loss. The damage was estimated at $3 million for the building and $1 million for personal property, including jewelry and fur coats. The grand Hotel Chamberlin was gone.

Chapter 6

REBIRTH

The blaze of March 7, 1920, sent an eerie glow across Hampton Roads. By morning, The Chamberlin was no more. The smoldering ruins created quite a sight. Curiosity seekers looked upon the rubble, and all were amazed that there were no fatalities. While several adjacent buildings had been destroyed by the fire, the Old Point Comfort Wharf escaped damage. Fort Monroe had lost its grand hotel, and many wondered if The Chamberlin would be rebuilt.

The hotel's owners, the Old Point Hotel Corporation, intended to reconstruct the hotel. Unfortunately, the company encountered financial difficulties. Fort Monroe's leadership did not want another hotel as it recognized the administrative and jurisdiction problems caused by the hotel's location on a military installation. Nevertheless, the War Department gave the Old Point Hotel Corporation approval to rebuild the hotel on April 30, 1926. The lease stipulated that work on the new building would have to begin within six months. An extension was granted for an additional six months. When April 30, 1927, dawned, Fort Monroe officials were preparing to contact the War Department with news that the project had failed to start. At 10:45 a.m., however, workmen broke ground on the project. Continued financial problems prompted the owners to seek and secure backing from the Vanderbilt Hotel Company.

The involvement of the Vanderbilts was to ensure that the new hotel on Old Point Comfort would maintain the high standards set by the Commodore Hotel in New York City. Marcellus Wright, a highly successful architect

Left: The Hotel Chamberlin ruins. *Courtesy of the Casemate Museum.*

Below: A stock certificate for the Old Point Comfort Hotel Corporation. *Courtesy of the Hampton History Museum.*

who had designed the John Marshall Hotel and Mosque Auditorium in Richmond, conceived the overall design. However, the Vanderbilts also used the services of Whitney Warren, of the firm Warren and Wetmore, as associate architect. This firm had an established reputation for hotel work and had designed several important New York City hotels, such as the Biltmore, the Ambassador and the Ritz Carlton, as well as the Homestead Hotel in Hot Springs. The architects expanded on the Georgian style. This decision was perhaps prompted by the hotel's location, an area rich in Colonial architecture (Rockefeller was just beginning his Colonial Williamsburg restoration project), as well as the Vanderbilts' deep interest in this style as evidenced by the new Vanderbilt Hotel in New York. Marcellus Wright and Whitney Warren combined to resolve the problems associated with the Georgian high-rise by concentrating ornamentation on the top and bottom stories, while the middle areas were generally neglected. They believed that "the Georgian was considered to project a relaxed air of hominess and family character, an image that a resort hotel on the Chesapeake Bay would be most eager to cultivate."

The Chamberlin is an example of a Beaux-Arts interpretation of the Georgian style. When completed in 1928, The Chamberlin Hotel rose nine stories above sea level. It was the largest building on Old Point Comfort and was very visible to boat and automobile traffic throughout Hampton Roads. Many travelers commented that when they arose in the morning aboard an Old Bay Line steamer, the first thing they could see as they approached Hampton Roads was The Chamberlin. Others noted how the morning sun shone off of The Chamberlin's windows, creating a shimmering beacon into the harbor.

The rebuilt Chamberlin Hotel. *Courtesy of the Casemate Museum.*

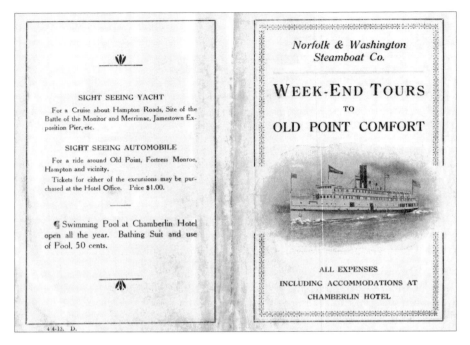

An advertising brochure for the Norfolk & Washington Steamboat Company. *Courtesy of the Hampton History Museum.*

The Chamberlin was constructed on a *U*-shaped pattern facing north. The front has a projecting central pavilion, topped with a pediment *en ressant*. The entry is centered on its own smaller pedimental pavilion that projects to the street. The cast stone pediment is supported by paired Doric pilasters. A pair of exterior stairs once led from Fenwick Road up to the main entry, formerly a pair of French doors centered below a multi-light transom, a pattern fanlight and a glazed semicircular arch with cast stone voussoirs. The stairs were removed in the early 1960s.

When the C&O Railroad closed its Old Point Station and the Old Bay Line ceased its operations, The Chamberlin had to rely on the automobile to bring guests to the hotel. Consequently, a ground floor entry was installed to accommodate guests who preferred to ascend to the main floor via elevator. The main entry on Fenwick Road is centered below an arched window with a patterned fanlight.

Much of the building's first floor, a raised basement, was designed to accommodate service functions. The most distinguished feature at this level is the indoor heated seawater swimming pool, built of multicolored mosaic tiles that indicate the pool's depth. Matching tiles wrap the columns that define the pool area. The remaining space was set aside for retail shops and offices.

The main floor of the north façade is articulated as an arcade, whose openings, save the last to the east, are filled with round arched windows. Each arch is flanked by paired Tuscan pilasters and is distinguished by stone voussoirs and carved keystones. The keystones rise to touch a stone entablature that runs the length of the ground-floor façade. To the west, the entablature is topped by a blocking course, while the rest of the arcade is topped by a metal balustrade, with stone supports arranged symmetrically and paired pilasters below. This level's interior is the most significant public space in the building. The wide corridor leads from the east terrace to the expansive lobby area. This generous corridor, flowed in black-and-white terrazzo, links the hotel's public spaces. The dining room's windows reveal an expansive view of Hampton Roads. Enclosed terraces flanking the south entry provide a protected space from which to watch passing ships. The east façade faces directly toward the Chesapeake Capes and the former site of the second Hygeia Hotel. This open space, featuring a band pavilion, is now known as Continental Park. The main-floor terrace disguises the Palladian windows. Pedimented bays occur every third bay, the northernmost of which provides an entry to the arcade by means of a three-dimensional staircase.

The main seven-story mass of the hotel is stepped back from the main floor and is generally a tripartite grouping of pavilions. The variation of the pattern of window openings provides a subtle relief to the massive guest room block. Two balconettes, located in the central bays on the seventh floor of the end pavilions, enliven the Flemish-bond façade. At the level of the windowsills on the eighth floor, a heavy stone string course griddles the lower section, while a medallioned entablature and horizontal cornice encircle the hotel at the top of the eighth floor.

The penthouse level is capped by a single entablature with a full pediment over the central pavilion. The tympanum is enlivened by an oculus, wreathed and swagged in a Georgian manner. This pediment is topped by a stepped attic, which hides a gable roof.

The end pavilions of the structure protrude on the southern side to create a *U*-shaped structure. The central portion of the south façade has a three-way staircase, leading to a pedimental center bay. At the ninth story, the two bays are adorned with pediments whose tympani are decorated with stone festoons and shields. A quoined tower rises above each pediment to a cornice with heavy medallions. Each tower is topped by a brick and stone parapet that once held a wooden cupola. An oculus decorates the

The Hotel Chamberlin. *Courtesy of John Moran Quarstein.*

wall between the pediment and cornice on three sides of the tower. The Chamberlin's top floor held the solarium and ballroom known as The Roof Garden. This area's rounded exterior wall is a series of French doors, all of which open onto a roof terrace. When the hotel was opened, The Roof Garden was promoted as the only one in the "Tidewater Section." The Roof Garden, with its glassed-in dining room and dance floor, afforded a magnificent view of Hampton Roads and the Chesapeake Bay. On clear nights, you could see the Cape Henry Light beckoning ships through the Virginia Capes. The building's height offered soothing breezes during the ever-popular summer dances.

The hotel was rapidly constructed, and the work was completed on April 7, 1928. It was eight years and one month after the fire that destroyed the original Chamberlin, and construction was accomplished just in time to welcome the Edison Illuminating Company for its annual meeting. The attendees were graced by a wondrous meal of Virginia ham, pork roast and scalloped oysters. Each stockholder received a paperweight made from iron recovered from the wreck of the Confederate ironclad CSS *Virginia* (*Merrimack*). The Chamberlin-Vanderbilt Hotel held its grand opening on February 11, 1929. It was a spectacular event.

The new Chamberlin dominated the Hampton Roads landscape. The inspiring Colonial design was lauded as a reflection of Tidewater Virginia's

Guests gather outside The Chamberlin. *Courtesy of the Hampton History Museum.*

historic background. The hotel was an imposing three-hundred-room, fireproof (obviously a reference to the 1920 fire) structure equipped with all of the luxuries, comforts and conveniences. Once again, Old Point Comfort was being promoted as a complete resort. The Chamberlin offered its guests golf, tennis, swimming (indoor and outdoor pools featuring purified salt water), boating, fishing, horseback riding, tours of nearby historic sites, seasonal waterfowl hunting and therapeutic treatments. All of these wonderful benefits were framed by "the atmosphere of Fortress Monroe with its brilliant gathering of officers of the Army, Navy, and Air Forces."

The Chamberlin-Vanderbilt Hotel was operated on the "American Plan," with food and service of the Vanderbilt standard. The meals, nonetheless, focused on traditional Chesapeake Bay recipes, featuring seafood, wild duck and other regional favorites.

Just as Harrison Phoebus advertised his Hygeia Hotel, The Chamberlin-Vanderbilt was promoted as a unique destination with excellent travel connections, noting that Old Point Comfort was "within a day's ride of half of the population of the United States." Steamships of the Old Dominion,

Old Bay and Chesapeake Lines brought tourists to the Baltimore Wharf. The Pennsylvania Railroad offered a train ride to Cape Charles, and from there a ferry took passengers to Old Point Comfort. The C&O also offered service to its Milepost 0 station at Old Point Comfort. The Chamberlin was indeed connected.

Success somewhat eluded The Chamberlin during the 1930s due to the Great Depression. Nature struck its own blow on August 22, 1933, when a large hurricane brought fierce winds and a high tide that washed over Fort Monroe. While The Chamberlin survived with little mishap, the post was severely damaged. The old bandstand, which had been the former bathing pavilion of the Hygeia Hotel, was completely destroyed. A new bandstand was built, and the Coast Artillery Band gave its first concert there on April 8, 1934.

As Fort Monroe went through a massive rehabilitation, several changes were made that had both direct and indirect impacts on The Chamberlin. The Baltimore Wharf, which had been battered by the storm and had lost much of its planking, was rebuilt.

Besides the massive repairs required by the 1933 hurricane, the 1930s witnessed tremendous improvements to Fort Monroe and prompted the demolition of the "other" hotel on Old Point Comfort, the Sherwood Inn. The Sherwood had been acquired by the U.S. Army during World War I. The building continued as officers' quarters until the completion of Randolph Hall in 1932. The Sherwood was then condemned and salvaged.

A Sherwood Inn clerk, circa 1910. *Courtesy of the Casemate Museum.*

Rebirth

Demolition of the Sherwood Inn. *Courtesy of the Casemate Museum.*

During the late 1930s, The Chamberlin was the only grand hotel on the lower Chesapeake Bay, and it became a virtual self-contained community. The hotel served travelers, vacationers and the local Hampton Roads community with lavish dining facilities, numerous leisure activities, a health club, a bar, concerts and dances. The hotel even had its own barbershop, bakery, ice-manufacturing machines and laundry facilities. The Chamberlin became the place for social interaction and summer fun. The hotel even installed slot machines, which became extremely popular.

G.T. Brooks recalled how his family used to spend the summers at their cottage on Buckroe Beach. Every Thursday, the mothers decided that it was their time to enjoy special "down time" away from their children. They would take the children to the Baltimore Wharf at Old Point Comfort, where they would purchase round-trip tickets on the Cape Charles Ferry. They would pay a "guardian" to keep the "kids in line," as well as the oldest child, a teenager named Billy Gooch. As soon as the ferry left the dock, the mothers would go into The Chamberlin to sip sherry and play the slots. When the children returned after several hours, the moms were all in a better mood. Gooch remembered that by the end of the summer, the fathers would join in on the fun, adding libations and dinner.

Gambling at The Chamberlin (there were always rumors of the on-going "big poker game" playing upstairs in one of the suites) was not well received

Inside the Hotel Chamberlin. *Courtesy of the Hampton History Museum.*

by the U.S. Army. The post adjutant, Captain Harrington Cockran, lobbied strenuously to remove the slot machines. After some maneuvering, he was successful and the slots were removed.

When the United States entered World War II, the entire Hampton Roads community was dedicated to war work. The tremendous influx of military personnel prompted the U.S. Navy Department to acquire The Chamberlin on January 1, 1942. Commissioned the USS *Hotel Chamberlin*, the building was purchased to provide housing for transient officers in the Fifth Naval District and the Chesapeake Bay Coastal Defense sector.

One of the notables to stay in the USS *Hotel Chamberlin* was Lieutenant Douglas Fairbanks Jr. Hampton resident Gwen Cummings remembered seeing Fairbanks and recalled thinking then (as she still does today) that "he was beautiful in his white uniform."

The hotel was operated by its former managers under the direction of the U.S. Navy. The building also underwent a significant structural change during the war. The twin grand cupolas that stood atop the building were removed by the War Department. It was feared that German submarines operating off the Virginia Capes would use these towers as a navigational aid. The cupolas were replaced by antiaircraft guns. They were removed when the conflict ended; however, the cupolas were never replaced.

When the war was over, several immediate changes occurred on Old Point Comfort. The U.S. Army terminated the Coast Artillery Corps and closed its school. The batteries already had all of their heavy guns scrapped. The fort immediately received a new mission as headquarters of the Army Ground Forces. This decision was made because of Fort Monroe's proximity to the Tactical Air Command headquarters at Langley Field. General Jacob L. Devers, commander of the Army Ground Forces, recommended this action; however, he also advocated that Fort Monroe needed more commissioned and noncommissioned officers' quarters, additional office space, accommodations for visitors and cafeteria facilities. Devers's solution was for the U.S. Army to secure The Chamberlin so that the two top floors could be used as office space. Other floors could be modified for use by assigned personnel and official transients, and food and recreational facilities could be provided on the lower floors. The War Department rejected Devers's proposal and recommended on July 1, 1946, that the property not be retained. Consequently, the hotel was sold to L.U. Noland on February 25, 1946.

Views of The Chamberlin. *Courtesy of the Hampton History Museum.*

Noland, who had various business interests on the Peninsula, including the Noland Company and Basic Construction, also operated the Richmond Hotels Corporation. This firm owned the famous John Marshall Hotel in Richmond and would eventually own the Americana House at Cape Charles, a popular resort built after the Chesapeake Bay Bridge Tunnel opened in the 1960s.

The Chamberlin returned to its former glory in the late 1940s. West Point cadet Jim Tormey, of Hampton, remembered that his first and best memory of The Chamberlin Hotel was from 1948:

> *That summer, cadets and midshipmen from West Point and Annapolis were involved in amphibious exercises at Little Creek...We were given passes on weekends; and, on this particular Saturday, General and Mrs. Bolte, the parents of my classmate, Phil Bolte, hosted a party at their beautiful quarters, overlooking the entrance to Hampton Roads. Also invited were some very attractive local girls. After dinner, we walked to the Hotel Chamberlin where we sat on the patio near the mimosa trees and listened to the band playing and watched the lights twinkling at Willoughby Spit across the water. I clearly remember thinking, "Lord, this is the most beautiful place on earth."*

The hotel appeared ready to once again become a major resort. The bay steamers continued to bring tourists to Old Point Comfort to enjoy the bay, sea breezes, Fort Monroe and nearby historical attractions, as well as other summer leisure activities. An outdoor saltwater swimming pool was constructed, and the hotel's interior was redecorated. Still the only grand hotel on the lower Chesapeake Bay, the *Daily Press*, on November 1, 1949, proclaimed that "The Chamberlin is almost a city all by itself, and a resort city at that." The Chamberlin was not just a place to stay on your way to somewhere else but a place to *be*.

The Chamberlin continued to expand its community role. Peninsula residents enjoyed "such activities as 'Beauty' shows, dog shows, antique shows, water shows, art shows, musical performances, and dances." To avoid Virginia liquor laws, the Chamberlin Club was organized to enable locals to enjoy a cocktail and a good meal. Two Broadway shows were produced in The Roof Garden, also called The Chamberlin Arena Theatre.

Old Point Comfort's last grand hotel was the social center for residents of the lower Peninsula during this era. Ann Tormey of Hampton (whose grandfather was one of the investors in The Chamberlin's reconstruction)

The Hotel Chamberlin swimming pool. *Courtesy of the Hampton History Museum.*

The Hotel Chamberlin's pool and tennis courts. *Courtesy of the Casemate Museum.*

remembered dining there with her family. "It was a treat," she reflected, "and we enjoyed flounder, crab, and oysters."

Ann and her lifelong friend Gwen Cummings learned how to swim in The Chamberlin's pool. Gwen's in-laws, Dan and Anna Lee Cummings, enjoyed Saturday evening dances in The Roof Garden. Her father-in-law would enjoy seeing friends and dancing the first dance. He would then go down to the pool to swim. Mr. Cummings would re-dress in time for the last dance. The Chamberlin was really something in the 1950s, Gwen Cummings reflects, "it was the Hampton's social focal point for special occasions, marriage receptions, and diners. It was its own destination," where one could attend shipyard launch parties and Christmas parties in the Noland Suite.

"It was just a wonderful place to go," Ross Kearney, Phoebus resident and former mayor of Hampton, remembers. "When I was younger, we used to take our boats out to Old Point Comfort to sneak into parties, and when I got older I enjoyed listening to bands like Terry and the Pirates and Adrian and the Sensations."

Bob Allsbrook remembers going to the Nachman's Bridal Fashion Show dance, perfectly dressed and driving his 1957 Bel Air Chevrolet convertible. He felt that he was "cool in every sense of the word." Everyone attending was dressed to perfection, and within the assembled throng he saw a tall, thin blonde whom he was determined to meet. When the opportunity presented itself, unfortunately, she ignored him. Despite this rejection, he would marry her fifteen months later, and he will never forget their meeting at The Chamberlin.

The hotel was a wonderful place to hold special events. Its grandeur made it the best setting for annual Christmas parties. The Hampton Kiwanis Club hosted a benefit for the children of Weaver's Orphanage. Other groups booked rooms so that attendees could look across the harbor and see the Atlantic Fleet aircraft carriers berthed at Sewell's Point.

Ross Kearney remembered that his uncle, Dr. Frank Kearney, was the hotel's "house doctor" in the 1940s and 1950s. Ross would pester him to see some of the stars who stayed in the penthouse suite. "Called Suite 200, it was lavish," he recalled, "the suite was on the end facing the harbor and included three sets of rooms on the right hallway. It featured a living room, dining room, kitchen and master bedroom, the size of three rooms." Ross pleaded with his uncle to allow him to tag along when Dr. Kearney went to treat movie star Jeff Chandler for strep throat. While Ross was not allowed to go, his uncle did bring back an autographed photo. Other luminaries who stayed in Suite 200 included Senator John F. Kennedy and Elvis Presley.

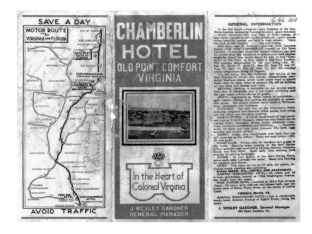

An ad for The Chamberlin.
Courtesy of the Hampton History Museum.

Unfortunately, America's travel and leisure habits were changing in the late 1950s and early 1960s. The Chamberlin was designed as a 1930s grand hotel and offered an opulent lifestyle. Ice water taps were in every room; however, even though the sea breezes stayed strong and refreshing throughout most of the summer, it did not have air conditioning. Travel methods also changed. America had taken to cars, and new road systems—including the Hampton Roads Bridge Tunnel, which opened in 1957—guided people past Old Point Comfort to Virginia Beach and the North Carolina Outer Banks. The Chamberlin endeavored to counter this trend.

Modifications were made to the building's north (main) entrance. The grand staircase, which once led to the main public area of the lobby, was removed, and a street-level entrance was constructed. Advertisements promoted the hotel as a perfect place "In the Heart of Colonial Virginia" to stop on a vacationer's way to Florida. The Chamberlin still continued to offer its "Health Studio" with "electric cabinet bath, intestinal irrigations and Manheim baths for heart and high blood pressure." The hotel also tried to connect itself to Virginia's storied past:

> In the Old South—Virginia—very Paradise of the Sun. White beaches washed by foaming breakers, green meadows—stately mansions—the lyric song of birds—canopy of blue skies—speech as soft as the golden air—great estates where beautiful women are held in high esteem. "Carry me back to Old Virginia"…not just a song.
>
> And then—one of America's greatest, most luxurious hotels—The New Chamberlin located at Old Point Comfort. It was here Virginians learned centuries ago that no matter what the variations in temperature might be

Approaching The Chamberlin. *Courtesy of the Hampton History Museum.*

inland, they would always be sure to find "Comforts" at Old Point, so they called it Old Point Comfort.

Despite all of the management's efforts; the sports; courteous, deft service; the tonic effect of seashore life; and wonderful Southern dishes, The Chamberlin was losing business.

In 1960, the C&O Railroad cancelled its passenger service to Old Point Comfort. The next year witnessed the end of the Old Bay Line steamship service. The Baltimore (often called Government) Wharf was condemned. The U.S. Army had relinquished control of the wharf in December 1959. The army had been striving to dispose of this structure since 1954; however, this action had been blocked by public outcry and legal obstacles. Old Point Comfort Wharf had been one of the busiest on the East Coast. It served steamers of all sizes, shipping out oysters and crabs, while receiving visitors and cargo. In the center of the wharf stood a building that housed the waiting rooms, the ticket office and mail and express storage. The Baltimore Wharf was once one of the lousiest wharves on the bay. By the late 1950s, the wharf had fallen into disrepair. The U.S. Army Corps of Engineers demolished the wharf in 1961.

The hotel tried to survive, relying on the "motor hotel" trade, and it began to depend on its connections with the military and local civilian community. Yet business continued to fade. The upper floors were left unoccupied, and

Dining at The Chamberlin. *Courtesy of the Casemate Museum.*

Old Point Comfort Wharf. *Courtesy of the Casemate Museum.*

Left: A Hygeia Hotel door key. *Courtesy of the Hampton History Museum.*

Below: The Chamberlin. *Courtesy of the Casemate Museum.*

the hotel completely closed weekdays during the winter. The Chamberlin's future seemed bleak. Then, York County businessman Vernon E. Stuart purchased the hotel for $95,000 in 1979, with the intent of restoring the hotel to its former grandeur.

Stuart spent $3.3 million; however, it was not enough to maintain and improve the structure. While business continued to fade, Stuart created The Chamberlin Museum, featuring items from the 170-year Old Point Comfort resort history. The Chamberlin was also listed on the National Register of Historic Places and was promoted as a Hampton Roads landmark. The U.S. Army even rented the seventh floor for office space.

In 1981, The Chamberlin missed out on international attention when it came in as second choice as the homecoming site for the U.S. hostages returning from Iran. Perhaps, this was a sign. Despite investing a fortune into the building, Stuart encountered tax problems, code violations and a tragic drop in use. In January 1998, Florida hotelier Jim Braggren purchased The Chamberlin from Stuart for $3 million. Everyone held their breath in hopes that The Chamberlin would be returned to its former glory.

Braggren had made his fortune providing linens, draperies and bedspreads to major hotel chains. He sold his company in 1985, and by the mid-1990s, he was purportedly bored. Braggren embarked on a spree of purchasing historic hotels, including the Palm Springs Racquet Club; the Willcox Inn in Aiken, South Carolina; and the Lakeside Inn in Mount Dora, Florida. The Chamberlin was the largest of his acquisitions; however, he called himself a "preservationist and restorationist" and pledged his project to "pay attention to details." Even though business increased at the hotel's restaurant, occupancy lagged.

Then, September 11, 2001, struck, and Fort Monroe was on lockdown. Visitors had difficulty accessing the hotel, and it was eventually abandoned by its owners. When Hurricane Isabel struck on September 18, 2003, the hotel's bottom floor flooded and water penetrated into various rooms, as well as the main lobby. The hotel was a wreck, and its future seemed very dim.

Chapter 7
OLD POINT RENAISSANCE

The old hotel sat vacant for several months after Hurricane Isabel. The storm had devastated the Hampton Roads region. This circumstance merely added to The Chamberlin's deteriorating situation. Many feared that this key Hampton Roads landmark would soon be lost.

Fortunately, Drucker & Falk, a major Hampton Roads real estate firm, took an interest in The Chamberlin in 1994 and decided to acquire the hotel. Drucker & Falk established OPC Hampton, LLC to manage the project, with the vision of transforming the historical building into a mature adult community. The concept was brilliant; however, the process of achieving a restored and vibrant facility would not be a simple task.

The project began with bankruptcy court and lawyers. The partnership had to deal with the former owners' creditors and to extend the lease from the U.S. Army. The lease process was arduous. It involved a change of use from hotel to apartments. While this process slowly moved forward, the U.S. Army decided to close Fort Monroe as an active post. OPC Hampton had to now deal with the Section 106 process concerning The Chamberlin's National Register of Historic Places status, as well as the newly organized Fort Monroe Federal Area Development Authority (FMFADA).

The mature adult community concept appeared to be the only viable approach to reviving The Chamberlin. The structure just could no longer exist as a hotel. The Chamberlin, according to John Munick, a former president of Drucker & Falk, had become "seedy in its last years." Even though it had once been a major destination, Munick reflected, "travel habits had

Details of The Chamberlin's
main dining room ceiling.
Courtesy of Drucker & Falk.

changed. The hotel rooms were too small and the furnishings were bad. The hotel did not meet modern standards and every recent attempt to restore the building had been underfunded. It was a sad situation."

Both Munick and Wendy Drucker, co-CEO of Drucker & Falk, had fond memories of The Chamberlin. Munick remembers the hotel as a grand social center. He and Wendy recalled the elegance of the dining room and Roof Garden and what a perfect place it was for weddings. He learned how to swim in The Chamberlin's pool, while Wendy met her lifelong best friend while participating in an AAM winter swim league based there. The pool would become a big focus for the restoration process. It had been neglected, and Drucker & Falk spent over $600,000 redoing the bottom. The ornate tile restoration effort was especially tedious, as each replacement had to be handmade to match the original. The end result was spectacular.

The Drucker & Falk team wanted to do everything just right as it was determined to revitalize the genteel lifestyle of the Old Point Comfort resort. The goal of providing modern living in a historical setting would return The Chamberlin to its former glory. Drucker & Falk hired Bob Mills and Bob Barnes of the Richmond firm Commonwealth Architects. This firm was well schooled in historic preservation. Mimi Sadler of Richmond was contracted to handle the historic tax credits component. Since The Chamberlin is listed on the National Register of Historic Places, the project qualified for state and federal tax credits, but only if the restoration followed National Register guidelines. Commonwealth Architects and Mimi Sadler worked with the Virginia Department of Historic Resources to ensure that key historical elements, such as the original mail chute and the dance floor, were retained. Larry Knox, who managed the project for OPC Hampton, noted that "about 35 to 40 percent of the renovation budget was spent on restoring historical items." The attention to detail brought Drucker & Falk and their project partner, Armada Hoffler, great dividends. The $54,000,000 project generated $21,015,009 in tax credits. John Munick noted that The Chamberlin could not have been restored without this benefit.

While the restoration did pay attention to every possible detail, the project could not achieve everything that OPC Hampton had hoped it would. The old elevators, with their hand-operated doors, had to be replaced. Commonwealth Architects had hoped to reconstruct the cupolas which were removed during World War II, but the $500,000 cost just could not be absorbed by the project.

Today, the end result is truly amazing. The Chamberlin's charming architectural details have been carefully preserved, and decorative finishes have been added or recreated. Of the building's 220,000 square feet, only 135,000 are dedicated to apartments. The rest is a spectacularly restored open space. The Chesapeake Dining Room was elegantly redone, with exquisite chandeliers, sconces and other revitalized details. The dance floor is restored and its woodwork glistens. The foyer is impressive. The original terrazzo floor has been returned to its former glory. This grand open space has rekindled the building's grandeur to what it once was when it originally opened as The Chamberlin-Vanderbilt Hotel in 1928.

Wendy Drucker and John Munick both agreed that the only viable future use for this National Register of Historic Places property was as an adult independent living community. The structure's location on historic Fort Monroe, breathtaking water views and grand architectural features made it a perfect venue for this use. Actually, the hotel had been home to several older ladies during the 1960s and onward. Mrs. Eubanks is one of the newest residents. Her mother lived as a widow in the hotel for several years, enjoying The Chamberlin's comforts.

Obviously, the restored Chamberlin's luxurious atmosphere, relaxed elegance and unique refinements make it a perfect place for an age fifty-five-plus facility. Besides the elegant apartments and rich architectural details, OPC Hampton partnered with Sentara Healthcare to offer a full variety of health, fitness and wellness programs. The restored heated swimming pool and the ability to walk along Old Point Comfort's seawalls and Fort Monroe's parapets provide residents a variety of recreational opportunities. It is well positioned to compete with other Hampton Roads senior living communities. Ask anyone who now calls it home—The Chamberlin is, indeed, *the* place to call home.

This page: Restoration details.
Courtesy of Drucker & Falk.

OPC Hampton's work returning the old hotel into one of Hampton Roads' iconic buildings is a classic example of adaptive reuse of a historical structure. Hampton's mayor, Molly Joseph Ward, recognizes that The Chamberlin is one of Old Point Comfort's signature properties and is a "symbol of how Fort Monroe's historic structures can be re-used when the U.S. Army leaves the post in 2011." Ross Kearney, a member of Hampton City Council and a Phoebus resident, considers The Chamberlin's preservation to be "a clear indicator that Old Point Comfort will once again be an important economic engine for our city."

The Chamberlin's transformation enables people to enjoy Old Point Comfort's resort traditions and the elegance of a grand hotel. Museum exhibits, created in conjunction with the Hampton History Museum, help connect residents, their guests and visitors with this resort heritage. Even a few ghost stories, no matter how improbable they might be, still linger throughout this historic structure. One is about Isabell. The tale begins with the March 7, 1920 fire that completely destroyed the original Chamberlin Hotel. Isabell was waiting in her room for her new husband, who had gone downstairs. Supposedly, when the fire broke out, the groom could not return to save her, and she perished in the blaze. In truth, no one died in this disastrous fire. Staff members of the old hotel remember the presence of perfume or a soft lamenting throughout the hallways or in various rooms. Perhaps it was Isabell.

The first Hotel Chamberlin during a hurricane. *Courtesy of the Hampton History Museum.*

The real stories of The Chamberlin are associated with its nearly two hundred years of legacy resort, maritime, transportation, military and social history. Whether the grand dances of the early 1900s or Edgar Allan Poe's last public recital, all of this heritage comes together when you walk up the east steps through the veranda and into the foyer. The views, architecture and history make The Chamberlin's renaissance an amazing story in itself.

The Chamberlin's veranda. *Courtesy of the Hampton History Museum.*

Over the past five decades, I have witnessed The Chamberlin evolve from one of the Peninsula's social centers into yet another sad, abandoned building. I visited this grand hotel often while I lived and worked on Fort Monroe. Everything about The Chamberlin back in the 1960s just seemed marvelous. The food (my favorite was the spoon bread) was always perfectly presented and deliciously prepared. Besides the fine dining, the hotel's architecture provided a grandeur that properly framed every event or activity. Whether antique shows, swimming or socializing, The Chamberlin was a place to enjoy.

All my time at The Chamberlin made me reflect on Old Point Comfort's resort heritage. After all, The Chamberlin was the last of the magnificent hotels that made Old Point Comfort into the South's most popular resort. Steamships and railroads brought thousands of people during the season to the Sherwood Inn, Hygeia Hotel and The Chamberlin. It all began with the first Hygeia in the 1820s. Old Point Comfort—with its views, access, history, recreational opportunities, fresh breezes and hospitality—was known as

Left: An old ad for The Chamberlin. *Courtesy of John Moran Quarstein.*

Below: Old Point Comfort guests observe an "ancient" Civil War–era cannon. *Courtesy of John Moran Quarstein.*

The view from The Chamberlin. *Courtesy of Drucker & Falk.*

"America's Resort" by 1900. With over two thousand hotel rooms, crowds clamored to be seen in the dancing pavilion or strolling along verandas. By 1928, only The Chamberlin, a brick edifice constructed to replace the original structure destroyed by fire, remained.

As I grew older, so did The Chamberlin. I continued to go there to teach Elderhostel programs or to attend the occasional social event; however, the building began to fade. Travelers wanted more, and The Chamberlin was transferred from one owner to the next. Each promised to restore the hotel's grandeur. Each faltered. Eventually, 9/11 made access virtually impossible, and Hurricane Isabel in 2003 flooded the bottom floor. The building was abandoned and seemed destined for demolition when a group of investors rescued the building. Thanks to The Chamberlin's National Register of Historic Places status, this over $50 million rehabilitation received tax credits and other incentives necessary to make the project viable. The Chamberlin reopened in 2008, offering unique historic apartments featuring panoramic views of the Chesapeake Bay, Hampton Roads and Fort Monroe.

The Chamberlin renaissance brings the Old Point Comfort resort story full circle. This beautifully restored historical building can once again carry on the health and hospitality traditions that once epitomized Old Point Comfort. I found the restoration so well done that I secured the two apartments where the old Book & Card Shop was located. I used the old exhibit cases to display memorabilia collected by my mother from Old Point Comfort. The two apartments were conjoined—one suite is my office and the other my living quarters. The architectural details, tall ceilings, Palladian windows and the Chesapeake Bay/Fort Monroe view sheds make this a perfect place for me to work and live. I am very proud to call this remarkable Virginia landmark home.

OLD POINT COMFORT RESORT RECIPES

E ach hotel that ever graced Old Point Comfort claimed that it featured the best cuisine. A review of the menus over the 180-year history of these luxury hotels offers insights into the eating habits of both gourmands and health seekers. Even though our eating habits and tastes have changed over the years, hotels like The Chamberlin offered nothing but the finest of foods, harvested from throughout the Hampton Roads region. During the nineteenth century, grilled canvasback breast, turtle soup and oysters were house specialties.

By the 1930s, The Chamberlin's meals focused on a classic Tidewater cuisine of various crab and oyster dishes, peanut soup and a variety of pork products like the traditional Virginia ham. This menu connected The Chamberlin's neocolonial design with adjacent historical sites, including Jamestown and Williamsburg. Food was indeed a connection and a statement.

I still fondly remember my first dinner at The Chamberlin. It was 1960. My family had just moved to Fort Monroe. My grandparents came down to Old Point Comfort on the Old Bay Line to help us acclimate ourselves to the new surroundings. We, of course, stayed at The Chamberlin. We went for a walk before dinner, and my grandfather enjoyed watching the ships lying in Hampton Roads and, more importantly, the fishermen catching flounders right off the seawall. He was determined to have flounder for dinner. I had no preconceived notions, other than anticipating a fine meal. My dinner dreams were immediately fulfilled when, right after being seated, a well-appointed waiter served us spoon bread, resplendent in a silver chafing dish. Oh my gosh! I could not have enough of this mouth-watering traditional

The second Chamberlin dining room, circa 1980. *Courtesy of the Hampton History Museum.*

The Sherwood Inn dining room, circa 1910. *Courtesy of the Casemate Museum.*

bread. The rest of the meal paled in comparison to that spoon bread. Many years later, The Chamberlin stopped serving spoon bread, and I still have not found another dining room throughout Virginia that could replicate this Old Point Comfort favorite.

My colleague Julia Clevenger and I set out to explore every aspect of the Old Point Comfort resort. As she helped me with the research and text, we kept finding references to the marvelous meals and classic seafood dishes offered by these hotels. Every menu we found or comments made by satisfied diners made us realize that we had to share some of the recipes we discovered. You may now enjoy the incomparable fare of the famous Hygeia and Chamberlin at your own table.

APPETIZERS
101

Hot Crab Dip   Bacon-Wrapped Scallops

DRINKS
103

Roman Punch   Hot Cider Toddy

SOUPS
104

Cherrystone Clam Soup   Old Point Comfort She-Crab
Peanut Soup   Soup
Tom's Cove Oyster Soup   Hampton Bar Oyster Stew
Terrapin Soup

POULTRY AND PORK
109

Roast Partridge, Quail or Wood Duck   Broiled Canvasback
Sauce Supreme   Cranberry Apple Stuffed Pork
                                        Loin

MEATS
112

Steak Old Point   Prime Rib Roast
Grilled Lamb with Brown Sugar Glaze   Old Point Beef Stew

SEAFOOD
116

Virginia Ham and Oyster Pie
Bluefish with Apples and Mushrooms
Crab Norfolk
Scalloped Oysters
Hampton Oysters
Clam Fritters

Stewed Oysters
Chesapeake Terrapin à la
    Chamberlin
Planked Shad Roe en Bordure
Deviled Crabs
Sturgeon Cutlets or Steaks

BREADS
123

Spoon Bread

Virginia Corn Bread

SIDES
124

New Potatoes in Cream
Yorkshire Pudding
Ham, Scalloped Potato and Leek
    Casserole

Potato Salad with Apples and
    Bacon
Deviled Eggs

VEGETABLES
128

Caramelized Onion Quiche
Buckroe Lima Beans
Fried Green Tomatoes
Hollandaise Sauce
Roasted Baby Carrots
Scalloped Turnips

Snow Peas with Pine Nuts and
    Mint
Summer Squash
Creamed Corn
Applesauce
Creamed Turnips

DESSERTS
136

Citron Cake
Steamed Chocolate Pudding
Foam Sauce

Strawberry Shortcake
Lemon Pie
Fresh Peach Crisp

Appetizers

The Old Point Comfort resort dining experience was always elegant. Inventories, photos, archaeological surveys and fond remembrances provide a glimpse of how the tables were set for special functions and everyday. The first Chamberlin used an anchor and crossed cannons to reflect its connection with the local military bases. The first Hygeia featured "Hygeia Hotel" emblazoned over a pastoral setting.

The place setting was complicated and connected to the meal that the patrons were about to consume. Each hotel had its own silver pattern and could offer a place setting for a five-course meal. The first Chamberlin's setting included a napkin ring; fish, olive, dinner, salad and cake forks; a service; meat, fish and butter knives; and dinner, soup, fruit and dessert spoons. Added to this array of flatwear, serving utensils were needed,

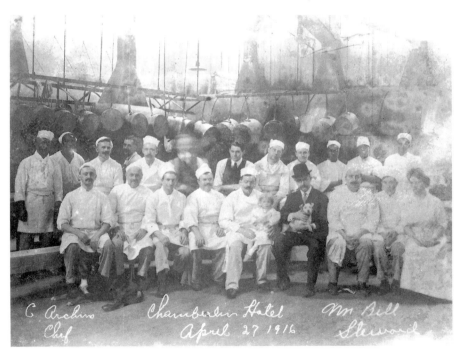

The Hotel Chamberlin kitchen staff, 1916. *Courtesy of the Casemate Museum.*

ranging from meat, poultry and fish forks to a melon knife, a soup ladle, asparagus tongs, grape scissors, a sugar sifter, a marrow spoon, salad scissors, cake knives, berry servers and carving knives. Several plates and bowls were required to properly serve all of this food. While consuming such a meal, patrons required white and red wine glasses, a champagne flute and a water tumbler to wash all the food down. Obviously, the stylized, purpose-designed eating tools matched the equally elaborate food.

Hot Crab Dip

1 stick butter, melted
5 shallots, chopped
8 ounces cream cheese
1 $\frac{1}{2}$ teaspoon paprika
Garlic powder (to taste)
Cayenne pepper (to taste)
Onion powder (to taste)
Salt (to taste)
Black pepper (to taste)
2 cups (1 pound) claw crabmeat

Sauté shallots in melted butter, add cream cheese and stir until melted and well blended. Add all dry ingredients and stir well. Add crabmeat. Cook over low heat, stirring constantly until crabmeat is heated through. Note: you may add a few drops of liquid crab boil.

Bacon-Wrapped Scallops

24 scallops
Bacon
Toothpicks
Brown sugar

Wrap scallops with bacon and skewer with toothpicks. Sprinkle brown sugar on top. Broil two to three minutes, flip and repeat.

Drinks

As a health resort, Old Point Comfort presented itself as having the purest air (the ozone layer was called "perfect for all"), the finest food and the freshest water. Water quality was indeed a great concern during the nineteenth century. The Chamberlin boasted of the unquestionable purity of its drinking water, as it was distilled and subject to the strictest sanitary regulations of the U.S. Army.

No dinner was complete at The Chamberlin without fine wines and cordials. Meals were served at the first Hygeia with two wines and champagne. President John Tyler and his wife, Julia Gardiner Tyler, organized several receptions at the Hygeia. One event, in honor of their first wedding anniversary, began with Roman punch, followed by immense hams and rounds of beef "à la Virginia." The meal concluded with apple toddy. Wine and champagne flowed like water throughout the engagement, with eight dozen bottles of champagne eagerly consumed by the celebrants.

Parlors at the Hotel Chamberlin. *Courtesy of the Hampton History Museum.*

Roman Punch

1 (50 milliliter) bottle of rum
1 (750 milliliter) bottle of champagne
½ cup curaçao
1 cup lemon juice
¾ cup orange juice
1 teaspoon grenadine
12 egg whites
Orange peels

Mix ingredients into a chilled punch bowl with a block of ice and add egg whites before serving. Garnish with orange peels. Serves about twenty.

Hot Cider Toddy

1 gallon apple cider
2 cups dark rum
15 whole cinnamon sticks

Combine all ingredients in a pot on the stove and heat to just below boiling. Serve warm.

Soups

John Chamberlin was able to secure a lease for a second hotel on Old Point Comfort thanks to the success of his Washington, D.C. restaurant, Chamberlin's. Chamberlin was a "gourmet of rare distinction." "No such place ever existed before, or will ever exist again," journalist Henry Walterson wrote. "It was the personality of John Chamberlin, pervasive yet invisible, exhaling a silent, welcoming radiance." Presidents, statesmen, diplomats

The Hotel Chamberlin kitchen, circa 1916. *Courtesy of the Casemate Museum.*

and millionaires sung Chamberlin's praises and feasted on food that "never a prince did before." His broiled canvasback, as well as mock turtle and terrapin soup, was considered the best the world had to offer.

John Chamberlin brought all of his restaurateur knowledge into the building of his Old Point Comfort hotel. The dining rooms were elegant and reflected the great meals he intended to serve. The kitchen "has frequently been pronounced by experts the most perfect to be found in any resort hotel in America. Nothing else could be expected in such a place of its magnitude and costly character."

Cherrystone Clam Soup

Cherrystone clams
Cold water
3 tablespoons olive oil
2 cloves garlic, minced
4 cups tomatoes, skinned and coarsely chopped
¼ cup dry white wine
1 cup water
¼ cup parsley, chopped

Wash and scrub clams well; discard any that are open. Soak clams for thirty minutes in cold water to cover. Heat oil in a large saucepan. Add garlic and sauté for one minute. Add tomatoes and wine and bring to a boil. Reduce heat to low and simmer for fifteen minutes. Keep tomato mixture warm while clams cook. Bring water to a boil in a large fry pan or Dutch oven with a close-fitting lid. Drain clams well and place in the pan. Cover and steam for five to ten minutes until clams open. Discard any that do not. Place clams in shells in heated soup bowls. Strain clam broth through cheesecloth. Combine clam broth and tomato sauce, mix well and pour over clams. Sprinkle with parsley and serve. May be served with crusty bread for dunking.

Peanut Soup

½ cup celery, chopped
¼ cup onion, chopped
2 tablespoons butter
1 can cream of chicken soup
⅓ cup peanut butter
1 soup can of milk
Peanuts, chopped

Cook celery and onion in butter until tender. Blend soup and peanut butter with vegetables until smooth. Add milk and simmer. Garnish with chopped peanuts.

Tom's Cove Oyster Soup

3 pints oysters
Salt (to taste)
Pepper (to taste)
1 stalk celery or pinch of celery seed
1 slice lean ham
1½ pints milk
2 eggs
Flour

3 tablespoons butter
Toast, cut into small squares

Pour oysters in a colander, put the strained liquid in a kettle and add enough water for quantity desired. Add salt, pepper, celery and ham. When the kettle boils, skim off the foam. Drop in the oysters, boil a few minutes and drop in the beaten eggs, milk and a little thickening of flour made with part of the milk. Add the butter and bring to a boil once, stirring to prevent the eggs from curdling. Remove from heat. Pour into a tureen over small squares of toast and serve immediately.

Terrapin Soup

1 pint terrapin (turtle) meat
1 quart chicken or white stock
$\frac{1}{2}$ teaspoon salt
1 blade of mace
$\frac{1}{2}$ teaspoon paprika
2 hardboiled egg yolks
1 cup hot cream
1 tablespoon rice flour
2 tablespoons butter
8 ounces hot Madeira or sherry

Simmer the terrapin meat for half an hour in the stock, adding the salt, mace and paprika. Mash the egg yolks until smooth and add to soup with the hot cream. Rub together the rice flour and butter until smooth, mix with a little of the hot liquor and stir into the soup. Let it boil a few minutes and add the rest of the wine. Serve with dry, plain, boiled rice, rice balls or egg balls.

Old Point Comfort She-Crab Soup

2 tablespoon butter
1 tablespoon all-purpose flour
1 quart milk
1 pound back-fin crabmeat

5 drops onion juice
¼ teaspoon mace
¼ teaspoon pepper
1 lemon rind, grated
½ teaspoon salt
6 tablespoons dry sherry
¼ pint heavy cream, whipped

In the top of a double boiler, melt the butter and blend with flour until smooth. While stirring constantly, slowly add the milk. Next, add the crabmeat, onion juice, mace, pepper, lemon rind and salt and cook over low heat for twenty minutes. Serve in warm cups with one tablespoon of sherry and a topping of whipped cream. Serves six.

Hampton Bar Oyster Stew

2 pints fresh oysters with liquid
2 cups water
2 potatoes, diced
¼ pound butter
1 cup sweet onion, chopped
¼ cup celery, chopped
½ cup green pepper, chopped
3 pints half-and-half
1 can evaporated milk
1 tablespoon Worcestershire sauce
1 teaspoon salt
½ teaspoon white pepper
⅛ teaspoon thyme
¼ teaspoon sweet basil
¼ teaspoon chives
Red pepper (to taste)

Drop oysters in two cups of salted boiling water for no longer than five minutes. Remove oysters and cook potatoes in the same liquid. Sauté onions, celery and green peppers in butter in a large saucepan. Add the oysters, half-and-half, evaporated milk, potatoes (with their liquid), Worcestershire sauce and the rest of the seasonings. Simmer briefly; *do not boil*. Let stand to blend flavors. When ready to serve, heat until hot but *not boiling*. Seasonings may be adjusted to taste. Serves eight to ten.

Poultry and Pork

President Andrew Jackson visited the Hygeia often during his sojourns at his "Summer White House on the Rip Raps." Hygeia owner Marshall Parks took great pains to provide the president with his favorite meals. Jackson enjoyed blackberries with milk, as well as a variety of fowl. His favorite was turkey hashed. This recipe instructed the cook to

> *cut up the remains of a roasted turkey: put into a stew pan with half a gill of sherry wine, shallots, truffles, mushrooms, chopped parsley, salt, pepper, two spoonfuls of aspic, and a little stock; boil half an hour, and reduce to a thick sauce; when ready, add a pound of anchovies and a squeeze of lemon; skim the sauce free from fat and serve altogether.*

Another president, Grover Cleveland, also visited the Old Point Comfort resort to enjoy duck hunting. The Chamberlin had its own hunting lodge and blinds on the Chickahominy River; however, Cleveland took a steamer to the Eastern Shore to enjoy canvasback shooting. Cleveland was a true gourmand and relished eating oysters followed by broiled canvasbacks. Old Point Comfort offered the perfect table for Cleveland's tastes.

Above, left: A Hygeia Hotel platter. *Courtesy of the Hampton History Museum.*

Above, right: A Hotel Chamberlin dinner plate, circa 1910. *Courtesy of the Hampton History Museum.*

Roast Partridge, Quail or Wood Duck

3 pounds dressed partridge, quail or wood duck
Flour, salt and pepper
2 cloves garlic, peeled and halved
¼ cup butter
1 cup dry sherry, white wine or chicken broth
1 tablespoon cornstarch
1 tablespoon water
1 tablespoon Dijon-style mustard
2 teaspoons red currant jelly
Salt (to taste)
Pepper (to taste)

Wash and dry the birds, and then rub with flour and sprinkle all over with salt and pepper. In a large frying pan, heat garlic cloves in butter until they sizzle. Add the birds and brown on all sides. Brown necks and giblets, too, if you have them. Put birds into deep casseroles along with the giblets and garlic cloves. Pour butter over birds. Pour sherry, wine or broth around birds. Roast uncovered at 350 degrees for forty-five minutes to one hour until juices run clear when birds are pierced with a fork. If birds look like they will get too dry, baste and cover with a casserole lid or foil. Remove birds onto a platter. Strain juices and bring them to a boil. Stir cornstarch with water and add to juices. Cook until thickened. Season with mustard and jelly. Add salt and pepper to taste. Pour the sauce over birds to glaze them.

Sauce Supreme

¼ cup butter
¼ cup flour
½ cup hot cream
1½ cups hot chicken stock
1 tablespoon mushroom liquor
¾ teaspoon lemon juice
Salt (to taste)
Pepper (to taste)

Put butter in a saucepan and stir until melted and bubbling. Add flour and stir until thoroughly blended. Gradually pour on the cream and stock, stirring constantly, and bring to the boiling point. Let boil for two minutes. (If a wire whisk is used, all the cream may be added at once.) After cooking, add remainder of ingredients.

Broiled Canvasback

1 canvasback duck
1 teaspoon salt
12 teaspoons pepper
1 tablespoon olive oil
½ gill maître d'hotel butter sauce
Watercress

After the duck has been dressed, singed and wiped thoroughly, split it through the back but without completely separating the pieces. Season with salt and pepper, and roll the duck well in olive oil. Broil for ten minutes on each side or longer if liked well done. Place it on a hot dish and cover with maitre d'hotel butter sauce. Add a bunch of watercress for decoration and serve very hot. Melted butter may be substituted for the oil. Ruddy ducks are cooked in the same way.

Cranberry Apple Stuffed Pork Loin

1 boneless pork loin (about 3 pounds)
Sea salt
Ground pepper
1 cup seasoned croutons
½ cup chicken stock
1 cup green apples, peeled and chopped
⅓ cup walnuts, chopped and toasted
⅓ cup dried cranberries
¼ cup shallots, minced
2 tablespoons pure maple syrup
1 teaspoon rosemary, minced

Preheat oven to 325 degrees. Rinse the pork and pat it dry. Butterfly the roast by first cutting lengthwise about halfway through it, and then angle the knife and cut horizontally almost all of the way through on both sides. Unfold the pork and cut tiny slits on the surface of the meat. Cover with two layers of plastic wrap. Pound with a meat mallet to flatten as much as possible. Remove plastic wrap. Sprinkle pork with salt and pepper and set aside. Place croutons and stock in a small bowl and let sit for five minutes, until the croutons have absorbed the stock and have softened. Mash the croutons with a fork. Stir in the apples, walnuts, cranberries, shallots, maple syrup and rosemary. Spread mixture over the surface of the pork. Starting with the smallest side of the meat, roll up tightly and secure with kitchen string. Coat the bottom of a roasting pan with cooking spray or a little olive oil. Place the roast in the pan and cook uncovered for about one hour and ten minutes, or until the pork reaches an internal temperature of 140 to 145 degrees. Start checking the internal temperature of the roast after about one hour. Let stand for ten minutes. Remove the kitchen string and slice into half-inch-thick slices. Serves six.

Meats

Hams, roasts and stews were popular fare at both the Hygeia and the Chamberlin Hotels. Specialty pork products were commonplace throughout the Tidewater region, and various types of hams and pork roasts would be featured during meals. Sometimes these meats would be mixed with seafood. One popular dish was scalloped ham and oysters. I remember enjoying chateaubriand, prime rib and various types of steaks—my favorite meals at The Chamberlin. However, I did not like to have my steak unless I had my shrimp cocktail or clams casino as well.

One advertisement from 1907 reflected that American tastes included a variety of meats. It appeared that The Chamberlin recognized that seafood and beef were a great combination. By the 1930s, beef was always a featured meal cooked in a southern style.

Steak Old Point

1 tablespoon butter
4 (3 ounces each) center-cut beef tenderloin medallions, trimmed of all fat
   and pounded to ½ inch thick, chilled
1½ ounces clarified butter
1 teaspoon Worcestershire sauce
2 tablespoons shallots, chopped fine
⅛ teaspoon garlic, minced
¼ cup mushroom caps, sliced ⅛ inch thick
1 tablespoon lemon juice, fresh squeezed
½ teaspoon salt (or to taste)
⅛ teaspoon ground black pepper (or to taste)
½ teaspoon thyme leaves, fresh
1 tablespoon parsley, chopped
1 teaspoon dry mustard powder
2 ounces heavy cream
1 tablespoon chives, chopped
1 ounce brandy

In a small eight- or ten-inch sauté pan, heat butter over medium heat for one minute. Add the tenderloin steaks, sprinkle with a little salt and pepper, increase heat to medium high and sauté for exactly two minutes on each side. Remove them to a plate and chill in a refrigerator for five minutes. Preheat a large sauté pan over medium heat for one minute. Add clarified butter and then Worcestershire sauce. Place the shallots, garlic and mushrooms in the center of the pan with the tenderloin steaks around the edges. With a spoon, stir and toss the mushroom mixture. After two minutes, add the lemon juice and season with salt and freshly ground black pepper. Turn the filet mignon steaks and add the thyme, chopped parsley and dried mustard powder. Cook the steaks to the doneness you like. Leave them in the pan and add the heavy cream and chives. Tilt the pan slightly and pour the brandy into the front edge of the pan. Turn the heat to high and let the flame catch the brandy's vapors and ignite it. Swirl slightly, turn off the heat and let the flame go out. Place the filet mignon medallions on plates and top with the sauce.

Grilled Lamb with Brown Sugar Glaze

¼ cup brown sugar
2 teaspoons ground ginger
2 teaspoons dried tarragon
1 teaspoon ground cinnamon
1 teaspoon ground black pepper
1 teaspoon garlic powder
½ teaspoon salt
4 lamb chops

In a medium bowl, mix the brown sugar, ginger, tarragon, cinnamon, pepper, garlic powder and salt. Rub the lamb chops with the seasonings and place on a plate. Cover and refrigerate for one hour. Preheat grill to high. Brush grill grate lightly with oil and arrange lamb chops on grill. Cook for five minutes on each side or to desired doneness.

Prime Rib Roast

3 teaspoons fresh ginger root, grated
⅓ cup orange marmalade
4 cloves garlic, minced
3 tablespoons soy sauce
2 tablespoons brown sugar
¼ teaspoon hot pepper sauce
1 tablespoon mustard powder
1 cup beer
1 (8 pound) prime rib roast
¼ cup olive oil
Ground black pepper (to taste)

Mix together the ginger, marmalade, garlic, soy sauce, brown sugar, hot sauce and mustard. Stir in the beer. Prick holes all over the roast with a two-pronged fork. Pour marinade over roast. Cover and refrigerate for at least two hours, basting at least twice. Preheat oven to 400 degrees. Place roast on a rack in a roasting pan. Pour about one cup of the marinade into the roasting pan and discard the remaining marinade. Pour olive oil over the roast and season with freshly ground black pepper. Insert a roasting thermometer into the middle of the roast, making sure that the thermometer does not touch any bone. Cover the roasting pan with aluminum foil and seal the edges tightly around the pan. Cook the roast for one hour in the preheated oven. After the first hour, remove the aluminum foil. Baste, reduce the heat to 325 degrees and continue roasting for one more hour. The thermometer reading should be at least 140 degrees for medium rare and 170 degrees for well done. Remove the roasting pan from the oven, place aluminum foil over the roast and let rest for about thirty minutes before slicing.

Old Point Beef Stew

2 pounds stew beef
2 tablespoons vegetable oil
2 cups water
1 tablespoon Worcestershire sauce
1 clove garlic, peeled
1 or 2 bay leaves
1 medium onion, sliced
1 teaspoon salt
1 teaspoon sugar
$^1\!/_2$ teaspoon pepper
$^1\!/_2$ teaspoon paprika
Dash ground allspice
3 large carrots, sliced
3 ribs celery, chopped
2 tablespoons cornstarch

In a frying pan, brown the meat in hot oil. Add the water, Worcestershire sauce, garlic, bay leaves, onion, salt, sugar, pepper, paprika and allspice. Cover and simmer for an hour and a half. Remove the bay leaves and garlic clove. Add carrots and celery. Cover and cook for forty to fifty minutes longer. To thicken the gravy, remove two cups of the hot liquid. Using a separate bowl, combine one-quarter cup water and cornstarch until smooth. Mix with a little hot liquid and return the mixture to the pot. Stir and cook until bubbly.

APPENDIX I

Seafood

Of course, The Chamberlin's cuisine was considered perfect—real Southern cooking specializing in fish, crabs and oysters right out of local waters. Advertisements beckoning travelers to Old Point Comfort could not express this truth any more than they did. The Hygeia's ads pictured this grand hotel as an inset to an oyster shell. The Hampton Roads seafood industry was in full stride by the time of The Chamberlin's construction. Hampton Bar oysters and blue crabs prepared in one hundred different ways offered guests true regional delicacies.

Oysters were always a staple on menus when in season. Other popular seafood dishes included clams, periwinkles, crabs, sturgeon, black and red drum, flounder, sturgeon caviar and turtle.

THE NEW HOTEL CHAMBERLIN AT OLD POINT COMFORT, VIRGINIA.—DRAWN BY HUGHSON HAWLEY.

The second Hotel Chamberlin. *Courtesy of the Casemate Museum.*

Virginia Ham and Oyster Pie

1 pint shucked oysters, drained
¼ pound cooked Virginia ham, cubed
3 tablespoons butter or margarine
2 cups fresh mushroom, sliced
½ cup onion, chopped
½ cup green onion, chopped
¼ cup flour
½ teaspoon salt
¼ teaspoon cayenne pepper
¼ cup parsley, chopped
2 tablespoons lemon juice

Biscuit Topping:
1½ cups flour
2¼ teaspoon baking powder
¼ teaspoon salt
3 tablespoons margarine or butter
½ cup milk

Preheat oven to 400 degrees. Dry oysters between absorbent paper. Fry diced ham in butter or margarine until heated through. Remove ham and drain. Add mushrooms, onions and green onion to butter and ham drippings in the frying pan. Cover and simmer for five minutes or until tender. Blend in flour, salt and pepper. Stir in oysters, ham, parsley and lemon juice. Grease a nine-inch pie plate. Turn the oyster mixture into the pie plate.

For biscuit topping, sift together flour, baking powder and salt. Cut in butter until mixture is like coarse crumbs. Add milk all at once. Mix to a soft dough. Turn onto a lightly floured surface. Knead gently five or six strokes and shape into a ball. Roll out to a nine-inch circle to fit on top of the pie plate. Cover the oysters with biscuit topping and score. Bake for twenty to twenty-five minutes or until topping is lightly browned. Serves six.

Bluefish with Apples and Mushrooms

1 bluefish
3 apples, peeled, cored and sliced
½ pound mushrooms, washed and sliced
⅓ cup water
2 tablespoons butter
Seasonings to taste

Put all ingredients in a baking dish. Bake in moderately heated oven for about twenty minutes. Serve.

Crab Norfolk

½ cup butter
1 pound lump crabmeat
½ teaspoon salt
¼ teaspoon pepper
Juice of 1 lemon
½ cup fresh parsley, chopped
Crusty French bread

Melt butter in a heavy skillet over low heat and add crabmeat, salt and pepper. Sauté gently, being careful not to shred the crabmeat. Add lemon juice and parsley and continue cooking until thoroughly heated. Remove from heat. Serve with crusty French bread pieces for dunking. Serves six.

Scalloped Oysters

1 pint fine cracker crumbs
¾ cup oyster juice
1 pint shucked oysters

Salt (to taste)
Pepper (to taste)
1 stick butter
1 egg
1 cup milk

Butter a deep earthen dish and put a layer of the cracker crumbs on the bottom. Wet this layer with some of the oyster juice and place a layer of oysters on top. Sprinkle with salt and pepper and lay small bits of butter on them. Add another layer of cracker crumbs and oyster juice, followed by the oysters, pepper, salt and butter. Repeat until the dish is full, with the top layer as cracker crumbs. Beat the egg in a cup of milk and turn over all. Cover the dish and bake for thirty to forty-five minutes. When baked through, uncover the top, set on the upper grate and brown. Serves six.

Hampton Oysters

⅓ cup butter
½ clove garlic, minced
1 small onion, chopped
½ medium green pepper, chopped
⅓ cup flour
Salt (to taste)
Pepper (to taste)
1 teaspoon paprika
1 quart fresh oysters
1 tablespoon lemon juice
1½ teaspoons Worcestershire sauce
Dash hot sauce
⅓ cup cracker crumbs

Melt the butter in a skillet. Add the garlic, onion and green pepper and sauté gently for three minutes. Remove from heat. Add the flour and stir until well mixed. Return to the heat and cook until light brown. Add the salt, pepper and paprika. Stir in the oyster juice, lemon juice, Worcestershire sauce and hot sauce. Mix until smooth. Add the oysters and pour into a buttered two-quart casserole. Sprinkle with crumbs. Bake at 400 degrees for twenty minutes.

Clam Fritters

50 small or 25 large sand clams, unshelled
1 pint wheat flour
3 eggs, beaten
½ pint sweet milk
Lard or beef fat

Take fifty small or twenty-five five large sand clams from their shells (if large, cut each in two). Place them on a thickly folded napkin. Put a pint bowl of wheat flour into a basin and add eggs, sweet milk and nearly a half pint of juice from the clams. Beat the batter until it is smooth and perfectly free of lumps and then stir in the clams. Put plenty of lard or beef fat into a thick-bottomed frying pan. Let it become boiling hot and then drop in the clam batter by the spoonful. Fry gently; when one side is a delicate brown, turn to the other.

Stewed Oysters

2 quarts oysters
1 cup hot water
Salt (to taste)
Pepper (to taste)
2 tablespoons butter
1 pint boiling milk
Oyster or cream crackers

Drain the juice from two quarts of oysters, mix in a small teacupful of hot water, add a little salt and pepper and set the mixture on the stove in a saucepan. Let it boil up once and then put in the oysters. Let them come to a boil, and when they "ruffle," add the butter. The instant the butter is melted and well mixed, put in a pint of boiling milk and take the saucepan from the fire. Serve hot with oyster or cream crackers. Serves six.

Chesapeake Terrapin à la Chamberlin

1 female terrapin
Flour (to desired consistency)
2 hardboiled egg yolks
⅓ pound butter
Salt (to taste)
Red pepper (to taste)
½ cup rich cream
8 ounces Madeira or sherry

Put a female terrapin in boiling water for five minutes to loosen the skin and then take it out, skin it and put it back in the hot water. When the claws are soft, it is sufficiently boiled. Take it out and remove the bottom shell first. Cut off the head. Take out the gall and sand bag and cut up the remainder. Cut up the entrails to half-inch long pieces. Be careful to preserve all of the juice. Put the pieces in a stew pan. Make a dressing of the flour, egg yolks, butter, salt, red pepper, rich cream and Madeira or sherry. Dish promptly and serve smoking hot.

Planked Shad Roe en Bordure

1 shad
4 shad roe
Salt (to taste)
Pepper (to taste)
½ stick butter
Parsley branches
Lemon, quartered

Butter a shad (fish), lay four shad roe on top, season with salt and pepper, put small bits of butter on top of each roe and set in the oven. After ten minutes, turn the roes over, make a bordure of a potato croquette mixture around the plank and return to the oven to cook until done. Pour a little salt and pepper mixed with butter on top and garnish with parsley in branches and quartered lemons.

Deviled Crabs

¹/₂ dozen fresh crabs
³/₄ cup bread crumbs
2 ounces butter
1 teaspoon mustard powder
1 tablespoon cream
Cayenne pepper (to taste)
Salt (to taste)

Separate the crabmeat from the shells. Put the crabmeat into a bowl and mix carefully with an equal amount of the bread crumbs. Work the butter to a light cream, mix in the mustard and then stir in, very carefully, a handful at a time, the mixed crabs, cream and crumbs. Season to taste with cayenne pepper and salt. Fill the crab shells with the mixture, sprinkle remaining bread crumbs over the tops, put three small pieces of butter on the top of each and brown them quickly in a hot oven. They will puff as they bake. A crab shell will hold the meat of two crabs. Half the quantity can be made.

Sturgeon Cutlets or Steaks

4 sturgeon
Salt (to taste)
¹/₂ stick butter
Cayenne pepper (to taste)
Lemon juice
1 cup bread crumbs

This is the most approved way of dressing sturgeon. Carefully take off the skin, as its oiliness will give the fish a strong and disagreeable taste when cooked. Cut from the tail piece slices about half an inch thick, rub them with salt and broil them over a clear fire of bright coals. Butter them, sprinkle them with cayenne pepper and send them to the table hot and garnished with sliced lemon (lemon juice is generally squeezed over them when eaten).

Breads

A second Hygeia napkin ring. *Courtesy of the Hampton History Museum.*

The Chamberlin conducted its dining according to the American Plan, which enabled the resort to offer the best cuisine and correct service at moderate prices. The menus were carefully selected, cooked and served "à la Chamberlin."

After John Chamberlin's death, The Chamberlin stressed that its meals were "just like you get at home; food that tastes good—old-time Virginia corn bread and Smithfield ham, oysters right out of the water; good, wholesome, American food, like mother used to cook."

Spoon Bread

3 cups milk
1 1/4 cups yellow cornmeal
3 eggs, beaten
1 teaspoon salt
1 3/4 teaspoon baking powder
2 tablespoons butter, melted

Measure the milk into a saucepan and bring to a boil. Add the cornmeal; cook and stir for several minutes, until the cornmeal has absorbed all of the milk. Remove from the heat and allow to cool for about one hour. The mixture will be very stiff. Preheat the oven to 375 degrees. Lightly grease a one-and-a-half-quart casserole dish. Place the cornmeal mixture into a large bowl. Stir in the eggs, salt, baking powder and butter. Pour into the prepared casserole dish. Bake for thirty-five minutes in the preheated oven or until the edges become lightly toasted. Serve hot, directly from the dish by the spoonful.

Virginia Corn Bread

1 cup flour
1 egg
³/₄ teaspoon sugar
1 cup yellow cornmeal
¹/₂ teaspoon salt
3 teaspoons baking powder
¹/₈ teaspoon baking soda
1¹/₂ cups buttermilk
1 teaspoon bacon fat

Preheat the oven to four hundred degrees. Mix the first eight ingredients together in medium-sized mixing bowl. Heat the bacon fat in an iron pan on the stove on medium heat. When the pan is good and hot, pour in the batter. Bake for twenty minutes. Butter the cornbread on top halfway through baking.

Sides

The Chamberlin bragged continually of its location in the great truck region of Virginia: "fresh vegetables are at hand, when other resorts are relying on the tin can." Side dishes featured a variety of new, sweet and white potatoes—all taken from "the rich, earthy goodness of Virginia soil."

The Hotel Chamberlin dining room, circa 1930. *Courtesy of the Hampton History Museum.*

New Potatoes in Cream

New potatoes
Milk (to taste)
Salt (to taste)
Pepper (to taste)
½ cup sugar
Flour (to desired consistency)
Water (to desired consistency)

Scrape and wash new potatoes, place them in a saucepan, cover with water and boil until tender. Pour off water immediately or potatoes will become mushy. Add milk, salt and pepper to desired taste and sprinkle the sugar over top. Bring to a boil and add a thickening of flour and water to bring the sauce to desired consistency. Cook until tender, about two or three minutes.

Yorkshire Pudding

1 cup all-purpose flour
1 cup whole milk
2 eggs
½ teaspoon salt
3 tablespoons beef or bacon drippings

In a large bowl, mix together the flour, milk, eggs and salt. Using an electric mixer, beat for five minutes, until smooth. Cover and refrigerate for one hour. Preheat the oven to 425 degrees. Coat a nine- by thirteen-inch baking pan with beef or bacon drippings. Preheat the pan for fifteen minutes so the drippings are hot and sizzling. Remove the mixture from the refrigerator, beat briefly and scoop it into the baking pan. Bake for twenty minutes. Lower the oven temperature to 375 degrees. Without opening the oven, continue baking fifteen minutes. The mixture should be puffed and golden brown. Remove from the oven and serve hot.

Ham, Scalloped Potato and Leek Casserole

4 cups potatoes, thinly sliced and pared
2 tablespoons flour
1 teaspoon parsley, diced
1 teaspoon chives, diced
1 teaspoon salt
⅛ teaspoon pepper
1 cup onion, sliced
2 cups cooked ham, chopped
1 leek, cleaned and thinly sliced
2–3 tablespoons butter, cut into 8 or 10 dots
Paprika and parsley for sprinkling

Preheat the oven to 375 degrees. Grease a two-quart covered casserole dish. Parboil the potato slices over medium heat in unsalted water for five minutes. Strain and replace the water with cold water to stop the cooking process. In a small bowl, blend together flour, parsley, chives, salt and pepper. Strain the potatoes. In the greased casserole dish, create multiple layers of the potatoes, onion slices, ham, leeks and a sprinkling of the dry ingredients in each layer. Dot each layer with some butter, reserving enough potatoes and butter for the top layer. Sprinkle the top with paprika and parsley. Cover the casserole and bake for forty-five minutes; uncover and continue baking for fifteen minutes. Serves four to six.

Potato Salad with Apples and Bacon

3 pounds small yellow Yukon Gold potatoes, quartered
Salt
5 strips bacon
1 large red or yellow onion, chopped
2 Golden Delicious apples, peeled, cored and cut in $\frac{1}{2}$-inch pieces
4 green onions, thinly sliced, including the greens
$\frac{1}{2}$ cup olive oil
$\frac{1}{4}$ cup red wine vinegar
$\frac{1}{4}$ cup Dijon mustard
1 tablespoon chopped fresh thyme or 1 teaspoon dried
$1\frac{1}{2}$ teaspoons pepper

Combine the potatoes and enough cold water to cover by a couple of inches in a large saucepan. Add a generous pinch of salt. Bring to a boil, lower the heat and cover the pan. Simmer for fifteen minutes or until the potatoes are tender when pierced with a fork. Drain well. While the potatoes are cooking, cook the bacon in a heavy-based skillet over medium heat. Once cooked, remove the bacon to a plate lined with paper towels. Reserve the bacon fat in the pan. Once the bacon is cool, chop it. Cook the onion in the fat in the pan on medium heat, until softened and just starting to brown, about five minutes. Use a slotted spoon to remove the onion from the pan to a large bowl and set aside. Add the chopped apple to the bowl. Add the potatoes and chopped bacon to the onions and apple. Add the green onions, olive oil, vinegar, mustard and thyme. Salt and pepper to taste. Serve either warm, at room temperature or cold. Serves eight.

Deviled Eggs

1 dozen eggs
1 teaspoon vinegar
Salt
2 teaspoons Dijon mustard
⅓ cup mayonnaise
1 tablespoon onion or shallot, minced
¼ teaspoon Tabasco
Pepper
Paprika

Fill a large saucepan halfway with water and gently add the eggs. Cover the eggs with at least one inch of water. Add a vinegar to the water (this will help prevent the egg whites from leaking if any of the shells crack while cooking). Add a pinch of salt to the water. Bring the water to a boil. Cover and remove from the heat. Let sit covered for twelve to fifteen minutes. Drain the hot water from the pan and run cold water over the eggs. Let sit in the cool water for a few minutes, changing the water if necessary to keep it cool. Peel the eggs. Using a sharp knife, slice each egg in half, lengthwise. Gently remove the yolk halves and place in a small mixing bowl. Arrange the egg white halves on a serving platter. Using a fork, mash up the yolks and add mustard, mayonnaise, onion, Tabasco and a sprinkling of salt and pepper. Spoon the egg yolk mixture into the egg white halves. Sprinkle with paprika. Makes two dozen deviled eggs.

Vegetables

The Hygeia Hotel welcomed a convention of vegetarians, physical culturalists and Christian scientists, as well as various naturopaths and food and health reformers, to an "Elementary" banquet on June 19, 1903. It was the first of its kind in America.

The first course was celery soup, served cold—it was said that stoves were a relic of barbarism—with olives and almonds. The second course

The Hotel Chamberlin's Easter menu.
Courtesy of the Hampton History Museum.

was a salad called "Brassica-Lactuca" of lettuce, stewed tomatoes, cucumbers and nuts. Vinegar was not used as it was considered dangerous by "Elementary" followers. Consequently, the salad was soaked with olive oil. The next course featured oat flakes and cream, pecans and brazil nuts, bread, sweet butter, fruit orza and raisatita. The bread was called "Crackers-Avena." It appeared like a small yellow brick. Crackers-Avena was made by grinding the grain, soaking it in water and then letting it dry in a form. The final course was called "Fructu-Salata"; its ingredients were sliced oranges, bananas, strawberries, figs, dates and other fruits. This salad was followed by Persian prunes, dried fruit, cream cheese and cantaloupes filled with ice cream.

While this was a novel meal, most dinners on Old Point Comfort featured locally produced vegetables. Creamed corn, asparagus, lima beans, carrots, parsnips, greens and string beans were prepared often in the French-style. Since roast pork was a popular main course, applesauce was always served. The pork was also supported with plain potatoes, mashed turnips and pickles. One menu noted Atlantic sea turtle soup followed by fried drum fillets and baked sturgeon.

Caramelized Onion Quiche

Recipe pie dough

Filling:
2–3 large red onions (about one pound total)
2 tablespoons olive oil
Salt
1 teaspoon balsamic vinegar
6 ounces (1½ cups) Gruyère cheese, grated
½ cup milk
½ cup heavy cream

3 large eggs
Pinch nutmeg
Freshly ground pepper

Pre-Baking the Crust:
On a lightly floured surface, roll the pie dough into a twelve-inch circle. Fit into a nine- by one-and-a-half-inch round tart pan, pressing dough into the corners. Transfer to the freezer and chill for thirty minutes. Preheat oven to 350 degrees. Line the pastry with parchment paper, wax paper or aluminum foil, pressing into the corners and edges. Fill at least two-thirds with baking weights—dried beans, rice or aluminum pie weights. Bake first for fifteen minutes, remove from the oven and let cool for a few minutes. Carefully remove the parchment paper and weights. Poke the bottom of the pie pan with the tongs of a fork and return to oven. Bake an additional ten minutes or until lightly golden. (Fork holes are for any air to escape.) Transfer to a wire rack to cool while making the filling.

Preparing the Filling:
Cut off the root end of the onions, so that the roots are cut but the hard core stays intact. Make a deeper cut on the other end of the onions. Remove the papery skins. Standing the onions root-side up, cut the onion in half. Take each half and make thin slices. Slice the onions in a way that keeps the segments attached to the root ends. The onions will take about an hour to cook before they are ready to go into the quiche. If you are making the entire quiche from scratch, it makes sense to get started on the onions once you've put the crust into the freezer to chill before pre-baking.

Heat the olive oil in a large, heavy-bottomed sauté pan on medium heat. Add the onions and sprinkle a little salt over them. Cook for ten minutes, stirring occasionally, until the onions have softened and are translucent. Reduce the heat to medium low and cook for an additional forty minutes, stirring occasionally, until the onions are well browned. Add the balsamic vinegar and cook for ten minutes more, until the onions are completely caramelized. Remove from heat.

Place the tart pan on a baking sheet to catch any run-off there might be. Sprinkle half of the cheese evenly over the bottom of the crust. Spread the onions over the cheese and then top with the remaining cheese. In a medium bowl, whisk together the milk, cream and eggs. Season with nutmeg, salt and pepper. Pour the mixture over the cheese. Transfer to the oven and bake until it is just set in the center, thirty to thirty-five minutes. Cool on a wire rack for about ten to fifteen minutes before slicing.

Buckroe Lima Beans

Butter
½ medium onion, finely chopped
1½ cups chicken broth
1 (16-ounce) package frozen baby lima beans

Heat a large saucepan over medium heat and line it with butter. Sauté the onions until they are soft and translucent. Pour in the chicken broth and bring to a boil. Add the lima beans and enough water to cover. Bring to a boil and then reduce heat to low, cover and simmer for thirty minutes, until beans are tender.

Fried Green Tomatoes

1 cup all-purpose flour
1 teaspoon salt
1 teaspoon pepper
1 cup crushed saltines
2 eggs, beaten
½ cup butter
5 green tomatoes, sliced ½-inch thick

In small bowl, stir together the flour, salt and pepper. Place the crushed saltine crackers in another bowl, and the beaten eggs in a third bowl. Melt the butter in a skillet over medium heat. Dip each tomato slice in the egg to coat and then dip in the flour mixture. Dip the floured tomato slice back into the egg and then into the cracker crumbs. Place the coated tomato slices in the hot skillet and fry until golden brown on each side, about three to five minutes per side. Add more butter to the pan if needed. Serve hot.

Hollandaise Sauce

3 egg yolks
½ lemon, juiced
1 teaspoon cold water

1 teaspoon salt
1 teaspoon ground black pepper
½ cup butter

In a small bowl, whisk together the egg yolks, lemon juice, cold water, salt and pepper. Melt the butter in a saucepan over low heat. Gradually whisk the yolk mixture into the butter. Continue whisking over low heat for eight minutes or until sauce is thickened. Serve immediately.

Roasted Baby Carrots

1½ pounds 5-inch baby carrots, washed
1 red onion, peeled and cut into 8 wedges
2 tablespoons olive oil
1 tablespoon fresh chopped rosemary or 1 teaspoon dried rosemary
Garlic powder
Salt
Pepper

Preheat the oven to 400 degrees. Gently toss together the carrots, red onion and rosemary with the olive oil. Lay out mixture on a rimmed baking pan. Sprinkle with garlic powder, salt and pepper. Roast for thirty to forty minutes on the middle or bottom rack, until well browned. Serves four.

Scalloped Turnips

4 tablespoons butter
½ cup onions, thinly sliced
4 cups turnips, peeled and sliced
2 tablespoons flour
1 teaspoon salt
Freshly ground pepper
1 cup milk
½ cup cream

Preheat the oven to 350 degrees. Butter a one-quart casserole. Melt one tablespoon butter in a frying pan and lightly sauté the onions until wilted. Layer one-third of the sliced turnips in the casserole dish. Top with one-third of the onion; sprinkle with two teaspoons flour, one-third teaspoon salt and one grind of pepper; and pat with dollops from one tablespoon of butter. Repeat this layering twice. Mix the milk and cream together and pour over the turnips. Cover and bake for thirty minutes. Remove the cover and bake for another thirty to forty-five minutes or until tender and bubbly. Serves four.

Snow Peas with Pine Nuts and Mint

2 tablespoons olive oil
½ pound snow peas, rinsed and dried, with tips of the ends cut off and strings removed
1 clove garlic, minced
¼ cup pine nuts
¼ teaspoon dark sesame oil
10 large mint leaves, chopped

Heat the olive oil in a large skillet on medium-high heat. Add the snow peas, garlic and pine nuts. Stir to coat with the oil. Cook for one to two minutes, stirring. Do not overcook the snow peas; they will get limp. They should still be a little bit crunchy. Remove from the heat. Stir in the sesame oil and chopped mint leaves. Serve immediately. Serves two to three.

Summer Squash

½ yellow onion, peeled and sliced
1 clove of garlic, chopped
2 pounds squash and/or zucchini, sliced
1 green bell pepper, seeds removed and sliced
Olive oil
Basil, either dry or chopped fresh
2 smallish tomatoes or one large tomato, peeled and cut into wedges
5 or 6 slices jack or cheddar cheese

Salt
Pepper

Put the onion, garlic, squash and bell pepper into a large saucepan with a couple of tablespoons of olive oil on high heat. Brown the vegetables slightly to enhance their flavor. As you are browning, sprinkle either dried basil or chopped fresh basil on the vegetables. When the vegetables are slightly browned, remove from heat, add the slices of cheese and cover the pan. In a separate stick-free frying pan, cook the tomatoes on medium-high heat for about five minutes, stirring occasionally. Let the juice from the tomatoes evaporate a bit. After five minutes, add the tomatoes to the rest of the vegetables and stir. Salt and pepper to taste. Serves four.

Creamed Corn

½ large onion, finely chopped
2 tablespoons butter
8 ears corn, husks and silk removed
⅔ cup water
1 teaspoon sugar
⅛ teaspoon nutmeg
½ cup heavy cream
Coarse salt
Freshly ground pepper

In a large saucepan, melt one tablespoon of the butter on medium heat. Add the chopped onions and cook for two to three minutes until translucent. While the onion is cooking, remove the kernels from the corn. Stand a corn cob vertically over a large, shallow pan (like a roasting pan). Using a sharp knife, use long, downward strokes to remove the kernels from the cob. Use the edge of a spoon to scrape the sides of the cob to remove any remaining pulp. Add the corn to the onions and butter in the saucepan. Add water and the remaining one tablespoon of butter. Bring to a simmer, reduce heat and cover. Cook for ten to fifteen minutes until the corn is tender. Add the sugar, nutmeg and heavy cream. Cook, uncovered, for five to six minutes, stirring occasionally. Add salt and pepper to taste. Serves six.

Applesauce

3 to 4 pounds apples, peeled, cored and quartered (use Golden Delicious, Granny Smith, Fuji, Jonathan, McIntosh or Gravenstein)
4 strips of lemon peel (use a vegetable peeler to strip 4 lengths)
3–4 tablespoons fresh lemon juice
3 inches cinnamon stick
1/4 cup dark brown sugar
Up to 1/4 cup white sugar
1 cup water
1/2 teaspoon salt

Put all of the ingredients into a large pot. Cover and bring to a boil. Lower the heat and simmer for twenty to thirty minutes. Remove from the heat. Remove the cinnamon stick and lemon peels and mash with a potato masher. Serve either hot or refrigerated. Note: this recipe is delicious with vanilla ice cream or vanilla yogurt and freezes easily (lasts up to one year in a cold freezer).

Creamed Turnips

3 pounds medium turnips
4 cups milk
1/2 cup heavy cream
1 large onion, chopped
3 tablespoons unsalted butter
1 tablespoon fresh thyme leaves or 1/2 teaspoon dried thyme
3/4 teaspoon salt
6 black peppercorns
6 whole cloves
2 bay leaves
3 tablespoons all-purpose flour
White pepper
Freshly grated nutmeg
Freshly ground pepper (optional)
Parsley (optional)

Peel and quarter the turnips. In a large saucepan of boiling salted water, cook the turnips until tender, fifteen to twenty minutes, and drain. In a heavy saucepan, bring the milk and cream to a simmer and keep hot over low heat. In a four-quart heavy kettle, cook the onions in butter over medium-low heat until softened. Add the thyme, salt, peppercorns, cloves and bay leaves and cook, stirring, for one minute. Add the flour and cook for three more minutes, stirring as you cook. Whisk in the hot milk mixture and bring to a boil over medium-high heat, whisking constantly to prevent lumps. Reduce the heat to a simmer, whisking occasionally for fifteen minutes. Pour sauce through a sieve into a large, heavy saucepan and discard solids. Stir in the white pepper and nutmeg and salt to taste. The turnips and sauce may be made one day ahead and kept separately in bowls, covered and chilled. Return the sauce to a simmer and add the turnips. Mash the turnips with a potato masher. Cook the mixture, covered, over medium-low heat for a few minutes. Serve with freshly ground pepper or parsley. Serves eight.

Desserts

The third course of grand nineteenth-century meals included a variety of sweets. Candied fruits, compotes, creams, cakes, pies, sweet jellies and candies were featured. Fig trees were found throughout Old Point Comfort during this era, and Hampton had a growing peach industry. These fruits found their way onto the tables of both the first and second Hygeias.

The third course was followed by a snack spread of radishes, cucumbers, celery, salad, cheeses, herbed butter and puddings. You were only supposed to eat until you were full; however, the richness of the food offered throughout these multicourse meals prompted many a dinner guest to need additional exercise.

An advertisement for the Hotel Chamberlin.
Courtesy of John Moran Quarstein.

Citron Cake

¼ pound butter
½ pound sugar
3 eggs, yolks and whites separated
½ pound flour
1½ teaspoon baking powder
1 tablespoon brandy
1 cup citron, thinly sliced and cut into strips

Cream the butter and sugar, adding sugar gradually. Stir in the yolks of the eggs, well beaten, the milk and the flour (mixed and sifted with baking powder). Beat the egg whites until stiff and add to the mixture, and then add the brandy and citron. Bake in a moderately heated oven for one hour.

Steamed Chocolate Pudding

1 cup sifted pastry flour
1½ teaspoon baking powder
½ teaspoon cinnamon
¼ teaspoon salt
1 egg
⅓ cup sugar
3 tablespoons melted butter
¼ cup milk
2 ounces chocolate, melted

Sift together the flour, baking powder, cinnamon and salt. Beat the yolk of the egg lightly and the egg white until dry. Beat the sugar into the yolk of egg. Add the butter and milk and stir into the first mixture. Stir in the chocolate and egg white. Serve.

Foam Sauce

1 cup butter
1 cups sugar
2 tablespoons brandy
½ pint boiling water

Beat the butter and sugar to cream. Add the brandy and flavor to taste. Pour the boiling water on the butter and sugar just before sending to the table.

Strawberry Shortcake

3 baskets of fresh strawberries
½ cup sugar
Whipping cream
Vanilla
Biscuits

Remove the stems from the strawberries. Slice into thin (one-quarter- to one-eighth-inch) slices and place in a large bowl. Add half or all of the sugar (depending on how sweet the strawberries are to begin with) and mix. Set aside at room temperature to macerate (the sugar will soften the strawberries and help release their juices). After the strawberries have been sitting for twenty minutes or so, take a potato masher and mash them a little, just enough to get more juice out of them. Whip the cream, adding a drop or two of vanilla and a teaspoon of sugar. To serve, break up one biscuit per person into big pieces in a bowl. Ladle the strawberries over the biscuit and add a dollop of whipped cream.

Lemon Pie

4 eggs
¾ cup sugar

2 tablespoons flour
1 ½ cups buttermilk
¼ cup butter, melted
Lemon peel, grated
3 tablespoons lemon juice
1 teaspoon vanilla
1 baked 9-inch pie shell
Cinnamon (optional)

In a large bowl, beat the eggs and sugar until light and lemon colored. Beat in the flour, followed by the buttermilk, melted butter, lemon peel, lemon juice and vanilla. Pour the mixture into the pie shell. If desired, sprinkle the top lightly with cinnamon. Bake in 375-degree oven for twenty-five minutes or until a knife inserted near the center comes out clean. Cool on a rack and serve.

Fresh Peach Crisp

2 ½ pounds fresh peaches, peeled and pitted
1 cup sifted all-purpose flour
1 cup sugar
¼ teaspoon salt
½ teaspoon cinnamon
½ cup soft butter

Butter an eight-inch square baking dish. Preheat the oven to 375 degrees. Slice the peeled, pitted peaches into the prepared baking dish. Sift together the flour, sugar, salt and cinnamon into a medium bowl. Cut the butter into the flour mixture with a pastry blender until the mixture resembles coarse meal. Sprinkle the crumbs evenly over the peaches in the baking dish. Bake for forty-five to fifty minutes, until the topping is golden brown and the peaches are tender. Serve peach crisp warm with cream or whipped topping.

Appendix II

THE COLONEL'S CAPITULATION

By Julian Street and Frank Finney

W hy did you follow me over here?" exclaimed Ethel crossly, as she began putting away her brushes. "You have made me nervous and spoiled my whole morning's work."

"I am very sorry," said the young officer penitently, "but I could not convince myself that all you said last night was true. I still hoped a little."

She closed her paint-box and folded her easel without making a reply, and he took them up in a matter-of-course way that suggested his familiarity with the task of fetching and carrying for her. But before they started to walk towards the hotel, she turned and looked him full in the face.

"Forgive me for being so irritable. I know you must feel very badly, and I blame myself very much."

"You have nothing with which to reproach yourself. I couldn't help loving you, and even though my dream has ended, I shall always look back to this month at Old Point Comfort as the happiest of my life."

"It has been very pleasant for me, too, and I am sorry it must end."

"But if you ever change your mind about devoting your whole life to art, may I not hope a little?"

"Oh, I'll never change my mind," she said, with decision; "you know we Burwells never do. I am just like grandpa in that."

In spite of the troubled state of his feelings, Jack Mallon laughed.

"I suppose it must be about time for his first drink now."

"If it isn't, you may rest assured that he will not take one a second before twelve o'clock," said Ethel, seizing the opportunity to change the conversation

"WHEN SHE COMES OUT TO TAKE TEA WITH US ON THE KEARSARGE"

to a lighter vein. With a last glance at the grey walls and green ramparts of the Fort reflected in the waters of the moat where she had been sketching, she took up her canvas and they strolled under the gnarled live oaks towards the arched entrance, where a sentry paused in his pacing back and forth to salute the officer.

"You feel sure that in all of his campaigns the Colonel has never taken a drink before noon?"

"Absolutely certain! It is a point of honor with him to keep up the family tradition."

"O! so there is a bit of tradition back of his custom."

"Indeed there is. The original Colonel Burwell, who settled in Virginia before the Revolution, had a theory that any man who drank before noon would die a drunkard, and made it a rule to allow no liquor to be served in his house before twelve o'clock. The custom has been kept up by the family ever since. That should be pretty good evidence to you that when the Burwell mind is once made up, it can't be changed."

"But have their clocks never stopped or gone wrong?"

"Indeed they have, and have been deliberately put wrong. It was to avoid a mishap of that sort that my honored ancestor had a sun-dial erected in his garden so that he couldn't be fooled. He used to say that you can push the hands of the clock ahead; but you can't push the sun."

"Then I suppose," Mallon commented whimsically, "that it is as hard to change the Burwell mind as it would be to push the sun ahead."

"Exactly."

"Well. In that case I shall not lose hope. The movement of the sun has been tampered with before."

"O! the age of miracles is past, and you are hardly a Joshua."

They both laughed at the comparison, for in his natty fatigue uniform he was as modern as could well be imagined and bore but little resemblance to the stern Hebrew warrior and miracle worker.

By this time they reached the hotel and Lieutenant Mallon said, as they walked up the sweeping approach to the wide entrance, "I suppose we may as well say good-bye now."

"What, are you going away?"

"You surely don't blame me if I run away for a little while after this."

"No-o," she said, with an unexpected clutch of pain at her heart. "It is all so unfortunate. But I am glad we are parting friends."

His hand touched hers for a moment and he turned away hastily without further speech. For some time he walked furiously on the pier, letting the ocean breeze beat against his face, but nothing could cool the fever of disappointment and rage against fate that was in his veins. Then, as is often the case when men are suffering most keenly, he began to laugh at his own position.

"Even an oyster may be crossed in love," he quoted, "and as this is the home of the oyster, I probably have all the company that my misery needs."

But the whimsical mood did not last. As his eye rested on the pleasure boats beating about Hampton Roads, he suddenly remembered the sails he had had with Ethel, and turned away, as if stung by the recollection. But the view in the other direction, though beautiful, was equally painful to him. He had strolled with her on the ramparts of the fort and on every

He Took Them Up in a Matter-of-Fact Way that
Suggested His Familiarity with the Task of
Fetching and Carrying for Her

LIEUTENANT JACK MALLON
A PORTRAIT BY ETHEL STAPLETON BURWELL

piazza of the hotel. Indeed, there was not a picturesque or historic spot within a radius of many miles that he had not visited with her. They had walked in the footsteps of the pioneers, and had even traced the wanderings of modern heroes and heroines of fiction, for the genius of romance is now peopling this storied and picturesque region with imaginary lovers.

She had sketched and he had applauded, and their talk had been of the associations of each place they had visited; of

Far-off, old, unhappy things
And battles long ago.

"Yet there is a sort of poetic justice in it all," he mused. "Her grandfather was a prisoner here during the Civil War and it was my father who was in command. Now she has me a prisoner, and I am being treated worse than the Colonel was."

Thinking of the Colonel, reminded him that he must bid him good-bye. As he expected, he found him in the Palm Garden, enjoying a cocktail.

"Join me," said the Colonel, promptly.

"No, thanks. My rule is not to take a drink until after twelve at night."

"That rule is better than mine. But sit down and tell me how your art education is coming on. I notice that Ethel gives you plenty of lectures."

"O, I guess my art education is finished."

"What's that?"

"It is for a while anyway, for I am going away this afternoon!"

The Colonel glared at him.

"Don't be a dashed fool!" he finally snorted. He had been watching the love-making with much approval, for this well-to-do, well-bred young officer was exactly the kind of husband he approved of for his favorite grand-daughter. He restrained his natural tendency to fly into a passion, and laid his hand gently on the young man's arm.

"Tell me about it."

"There isn't much to tell," said Jack, with an uneasy little laugh. "She simply won't have me."

"And you give up!" he roared. "Gad, sir, when I was your age a woman's 'no' only spurred me on."

"But perhaps you were never in love with a woman who was wedded to her art."

"Art be blowed! I'll find some way to knock that nonsense out of her head! The little simpleton!"

"Don't," said Jack. "I have learned to respect her ambition and desire to lead her own life, and do not feel that I have any right to pester her anymore!"

"Idiot!" snorted the Colonel.

"And then she has made up her mind about it, and you know yourself that when the Burwell mind is made up, it is as easy to push the sun as to change it."

"O, she told you that, did she! Huh!"

"And she says she has inherited your firmness of mind."

"Huh!" The exclamation and the glare that accompanied it boded a lively interview for Miss Ethel.

"Perhaps if you changed your mind, she might change hers."

"See here, young man," exclaimed the Colonel suspiciously. "This isn't another trick to make me break the family rule, is it?"

"Certainly not."

"You will pardon me for being suspicious," he grumbled, "but I have learned that you officers at Fort Monroe and the officers of the White Squadron have a competition on."

"Quite true," laughed Mallon. "We have agreed that whichever branch of the service induces you to take a drink before noon is to have a dinner at the expense of the other."

"Huh!" snorted the Colonel, "and all except you have been pestering the life out of me with tricky schemes. But you can't fool me by setting your watches back and getting the hotel clocks stopped. Just look on the railing behind you!"

Jack looked, but saw nothing that conveyed any meaning to him. He then looked enquiringly at the Colonel.

"Don't you see that mark there? That is where the shadow is at noon, and until you get enough engineering skill to push the sun, you can't trick me!" He chuckled.

"But we may catch you on a rainy day."

"Pouf! It's always sunny here at Old Point Comfort. If it wasn't I wouldn't bring my rheumatic bones here every year to rest and recuperate."

"Well, I must say I hope someone succeeds in tricking you, because that might enable me to make Ethel change her mind."

"Don't be an idiot!" the Colonel roared again. "It is a woman's glorious privilege to be able to change her mind. You go out to the golf links and have a game, and I'll have a talk with that young fool."

"Please don't," said Mallon. "She is feeling hurt over the matter now, and I don't want to cause her further pain. An I must really say good-bye to you now."

He arose and extended his hand.

"Well, leave me your address anyway."

"O, I feel in the humor for killing something, and I am going up to the Hotel Game Preserve for a few days' hunting. The Colonel gave me leave this morning."

"Huh! Well I am sorry you feel forced to run away."

"So am I. I feel as Adam must have felt when he was turned out of Eden—the only difference being that Eve refuses to come with me."

"Huh!"

They shook hands and parted, and the Colonel sat down to think, and his thoughts were punctuated with exclamations of the kind usually associated with retired military men. Presently Ethel came down from her room to see that all was well with him, and his experienced eye saw at once that she had been crying. Although his first impulse was to issue commands in military fashion, he refrained, and instead of roaring, used the soft pedal on his voice.

"Well, little one, what have you been doing all morning?"

"Painting."

"Huh!"

"I am trying to reconstruct the scene of Gun 40. You know about it, of course. It was where it stood in the old Water Battery that lovers used to meet."

"Your grandmother was sitting on it when I proposed to her," said the Colonel. "I wonder if your picture will be as I remember it. I can still see the grim old gun in the moonlight and can hear the water beating against the ramparts. I had just graduated from West Point, full of ambition, and she was very beautiful. Ah, my dear, you must remember while painting, that Old Gun 40 is reminiscent of love, rather than of war."

Something in his tone, together with the state of her own heart, brought the tears to Ethel's eyes. It was not a time for speech. She stooped impulsively and kissed him on the cheek.

"Your Grandmother was Sitting on It When I Proposed to Her"

There were tears in the eyes of the grizzled veteran as he looked up to her.

"You are very like her," he said brokenly.

She took his wrinkled hand in hers and stroked it gently. There was a silence that both seemed loath to break. Finally the Colonel murmured.

"Love is the only thing in the world that is worthwhile."

The tension was broken instantly. Laughing excitedly, Ethel exclaimed.

"That from you—from a man of war—O, that is too much!"

"Someday you will know," and the Colonel smiled foolishly.

"Nonsense! I have made up my mind about my life and love is not in the scheme of things for me—except love for my foolish old bear of a grand-dad." And she patted his hand softly.

"You are very young," he said absently.

She bristled up at once.

"I am at least old enough to know my own mind, and I know it."

"Huh!"

"Besides, I have made up my mind, and you know that when the Burnwell mind is once made up, it can't be changed."

"Nonsense! That only applies to the men of the family."

"But, grandpa, can't you realize what my art means to me? I couldn't love any man well enough to give it up. It is my life. And I never felt that more than since we came here—to this place that is the cradle of the greatest nation the world has ever known. This is the land of Pocahontas and the heroic pioneers of Jamestown, as well as the theatre of the Revolution and the Civil War. Every inch of it has a history, and as I transfer its picturesque scenes and the wonderful colors of its foliage to my canvas, I feel the spirit of my country thrilling to my finger-tips. When I sit at night and listen to the lapping of the sea, it seems to whisper of the marvel and mystery of the South. Everything here inspires and delights."

The Colonel said nothing. But he was wise enough to see that her enthusiasm was but a shield to cover a disquietude in her heart. Finally he said:

"You will forgive an old man, who wants to see his little girl happy, won't you?"

She froze instantly.

"Did he tell you?" she asked.

"I guessed," he said unblushingly, and the Recording Angel smiled and failed to record the white lie.

"I could almost change my mind to convince you that you should change yours," he continued.

"Then I am safe," she said, "for I am sure you never will. But I must go now, for you know I have an appointment with Lieutenant Pickton of the Kearsarge, to paint him in his uniform this afternoon, and I must get out the sketches I have already made."

"Huh! I wouldn't give much for his uniform when you get through with it."

"O, I am not collecting any more souvenirs."

"Well, it has lately come your turn to stop. The way you girls at this hotel rob the Army of gold braid and buttons, and the Navy of hatbands and rating badges, is something scandalous."

"But I have reformed," laughed Ethel, as she hurried back to her room.

When she reappeared in the Sun Parlor, she was accompanied by a handsome young officer in navy uniform. With much chaffing she got him posed to her taste in one of the easy chairs.

"Military men make the best models in the world!" she finally exclaimed. "Your discipline has trained you to keeping still when it is necessary."

"You can have me for a model all your life," he retorted in a bantering tone that was not all banter.

"Don't talk nonsense," Ethel said curtly.

"I don't mean it for nonsense," urged Pickton, seizing the opportunity of Lieutenant Mallon's unexpected absence to plead his own case. "I have been wanting to tell you for weeks past that I love you, but something always interfered or interrupted—"

But the poor fellow was doomed to one more disappointment. A band from the visiting English ship that was serenading the American Admiral stopping at the Chamberlin, struck up "The Star Spangled Banner," and with a look of ludicrous distress on his eager flushed face, Lieutenant Pickton sprang to his feet, as all military men must on such occasions. Despite the state of his heart, he stood still as a statue until the last note had sounded—and then it was impossible to resume his proposal.

Ethel smiled at the interruption and welcomed it. After such a break she did not need to reply unless his renewed his pleadings, and that he could not do.

The Saturday Night Dance

But what had happened to these men anyway? Couldn't they be agreeable to a girl, without making love to her? Two proposals in twenty-four hours would have been a record even for a conventional summer girl, but to a serious-minded maid with a purpose in life, it was simply a nuisance. Then, in spite of herself, she realized how much she missed having Jack at her side, chatting while she was at work. It was dawning on her mind that the parting meant more than she had thought. Once more her work began to go wrong, and it was a positive relief when the guests began to flock into the room in friendly groups to enjoy their afternoon tea. A quartette from the Hampton School began singing old-plantation melodies, and brisk attendants hurried about serving tea in dainty china. Her day's work was really ended, for the sun was already sinking, flushing the west with gold, and gleaming on the white sails of the ships in Hampton Roads. With a sigh at the hopelessness of reproducing such beauty on canvas, she put away her sketch before they could come to criticize or praise it, and presently a group of officers and ladies came and joined them.

"See her, Pickton," exclaimed an army officer, "you fellows may as well get ready to order that dinner. We have got the scheme to make the Colonel break his rule. And you had better get ready to go down deep in your pockets, too, for we are going to bring to your dinner all the officers in the Post and Artillery School, as well!"

"O," said Pickton, "we've got you beaten at that game! We are going to invite all the officers of the Squadron, the officers of the English ship that came in this morning, the fellows from the Receiving Ship 'Franklin,' and all the officers at the Navy Yard and at Newport News."

"Have you got a Svengali among you who will hypnotize him?" asked Ethel.

"O, we've got a better scheme than that. Some day when we find you sketching in the Fort, or when you come over to one of our dances or blowouts at the club, we are going to take you prisoner and hold you to ransom. Our ransom will be that the Colonel come over to the club in the morning and have a drink."

"If you try that, we'll blow your Fort off the earth and rescue her," said Pickton. "But I'm glad you told of your scheme, because we can probably forestall you by making her a prisoner when she comes out to take tea with us on the Kearsarge to-morrow afternoon."

"I'll bet the Navy wins in this competition!" exclaimed one of the young ladies in the group.

"Done!" exclaimed the Army officer. "Shall it be gloves or candies?"

In a moment they were all betting on their favorites; all except Ethel.

"If it were not considered unsportsmanlike to be on a sure thing," she said, "I would bet on the Colonel's firmness of mind. Both the Army and Navy will fail in this case."

In spite of her protest, she was forced into making several bets, and so with much banter and enjoyment the daily function came to an end, as the Army officers hurried away to prepare for dress parade while those of the Navy, being interested only as spectators, strolled over more leisurely with the ladies to view the ceremony and listen to the music of the Artillery band.

After Ethel had left him the Colonel sat and thought for a long time, and finally concluded his meditations with a particularly explosive, "Huh!"

He had looked forward to Ethel's marriage to Lieutenant Mallon as something that would help heal many ancient wounds. He could forget his treatment in the old prison, if the son of his jailer made the pet of his old age happy, and he did not propose to give up. At lunch Ethel kept up a chatter of conversation that made it impossible for the Colonel to speak out what he had on his mind, and at dinner they were joined by a couple of his old cronies with whom he fought over several battles with all his fire and energy. He hoped to catch her alone before the ball began in the evening, but could not manage it, though he constantly had the matter on his mind, for when it came to match-making, the Colonel had more persistence than a dowager. But while he moved about among the guests in the corridors and ballroom, exchanging old-fashioned gallantries with the beautifully gowned ladies, and saluting the officers, whose brilliant uniforms gave the ever-changing scene the colors of a musical fairyland, he kept constant watch on her.

He intended talking to her very frankly; but the opportunity did not offer that night, for when the ball was over, Ethel accompanied a party that visited the Army Club to enjoy the Saturday night hospitality of the officers in their unique club-rooms. But he divined from her feverish gayety that Mallon's departure had awakened her to the fact that she was every inch a woman, and that love cannot be gain-said. That settled everything for him, and led to the greatest sensation the social life of Old Point Comfort and the Hotel Chamberlin had ever known.

PRESENTLY A GROUP OF OFFICERS AND LADIES CAME
AND JOINED THEM

On Monday morning the Colonel stalked stiffly into the rotunda of the hotel. Several of his old cronies and a group of young officers were standing by the clerk's desk. They saluted promptly.

"Come and have a drink," rumbled the Colonel, returning their salute.

They all instantly glanced at the clock. It marked 10 A.M.

"Pardon me, Colonel," said a quick-witted lieutenant of artillery, "I have a couple of friends from the Kearsarge here, and I'd like them to meet you."

"Huh! Bring them along." The Colonel knew that meant the settling of the competition, and a subsequent dinner. When the introductions had been made, he led the way to Palm Garden. An attentive colored boy took their orders.

He Knew of a Particular Corner of the Pavilion — Over the Sea — and There He Found Her

"My usual cocktail," said the Colonel when the others had given their orders, "and when you have served it, go up to Miss Ethel's room and tell her I wish to see her here."

While they were enjoying their drinks and the Army men were slyly chaffing their disconsolate friends of the Navy, Ethel appeared.

She bowed to the officers and the Colonel raised his glass.

"To you happiness!"

"Why, grandpa," she gasped—and then she understood.

"Pardon me," she said to the merry company, and bowing in a dazed matter, she fled to her room. As soon as might be, the Colonel dismissed his friends and moved with his accustomed dignity to the telegraph office. Here he dispatched the following telegram:

Lieutenant Jack Mallon,
Chamberlin Game Preserve
Toano, Va.
It is now ten a.m. I have just had a cocktail. The Burwell mind can be
changed. Come back.
Colonel Burwell

When Jack returned, Ethel was nowhere to be seen. But he knew of a particular corner of the pavilion, out over the sea, where they had often watched the shifting panorama of searchlights and passing vessels, finding new charms in every change of the scene, whether by day or night, by moonlight or in the starry darkness. It was there that they had had their most intimate conversations, and there he found her. On their privacy the world has no right to intrude.

***

The wedding at the Old Post Chapel, at the height of the season, was conducted with the fullest military honors. The church was decorated with the blue and gold of the Navy, and the scarlet and blue of the Artillery.

HOTEL CHAMBERLIN

Two of the ushers were Navy officers, and two were officers from the Post. The Colonel donned his old uniform to give his favorite away and the whole scene was one to delight the artistic sense of the beautiful bride.

At the wedding breakfast that followed at The Chamberlin, the Commanding Officer of the Post honored the young couple by proposing the health of the bride. When he had completed his compliments and called on all to drink, the Colonel stood up, but before drinking, ostentatiously looked at his watch to make sure that it was past twelve o'clock.

"But why this carefulness?" said the happy bridegroom. "You have broken your rule anyway."

"Huh! You are mistaken. I never have."

"But I drank with you," said an officer.

"Our rule," said the Colonel, "doesn't say how late we may drink, but how early. On that occasion I had sat up all night, and that drink belonged to the day before."

When the laughter subsided, a Navy officer exclaimed:

"We have been tricked out of a dinner. To make things square, the Army must give the Navy one."

"If they won't pay for it, I will!" exclaimed Jack.

"Oh, we'll give a dinner all right, and you can give another."

"Agreed!"

And the Colonel who had out-generaled them all glared about him, then beamed on Mrs. Mallon and said:

"Huh!"

ABOUT THE AUTHORS

John V. Quarstein is an award-winning historian, author and preservationist. He serves on several national organizations such as the Fort Monroe Federal Area Development Authority, the Virginia Sesquicentennial Commission's Advisory Council and the Virginia Civil War Trails. After serving for thirty years as director of the Virginia War Museum, he presently works as historian for the City of Hampton, Virginia, and is president of the Quarstein Foundation. Quarstein is the author of nine books and has created five PBS documentaries. He resides in the historic Chamberlin Hotel at Fort Monroe, Virginia, and at his Eastern Shore farm. In his spare time, he is an avid duck hunter and collector of decoys and antique shotguns.

Julia Steere Clevenger works as the program manager for the Quarstein Foundation located in Hampton, Virginia. She serves on several state and nonprofit boards, including the Cedar Creek Battlefield Foundation and the Lord Fairfax Community College Educational Foundation Board. She also serves on the Hampton/Winchester Virginia Sesquicentennial Committees. Julia is an active advocate and lobbyist for the National MS Society in Virginia and is the mother of three children. She enjoys spending her free time working on volunteer projects, biking and traveling.

All proceeds from the sale of *Old Point Comfort Resort: Hospitality, Health and History on Virginia's Chesapeake Bay* will be contributed to Old Point Comfort Conservancy. This nonprofit foundation was established to ensure the preservation and interpretation of Fort Monroe's historical structures. The conservancy's offices can be found in The Chamberlin. For more information, write:

Old Point Comfort Conservancy
2 Fenwick Road
Suite 201
Fort Monroe, VA 23651